Vegetable

Vegetable Gardener's Bible: 5 in 1 Create a Sustainable Food Source at Home with Cutting-Edge Urban Farming Strategies

Sierra Caldwell

Book I: Foundations of Urban Garden

Hydroponics: The Soilless Wonder

Optimizing Plant Health and Yield

Book III: Ecological Pest and Disease Management

Understanding and Preventing Pests and Diseases

Winter: Planning and Preparation

Book V: Beyond the Garden

Harvest and Preservation

Community and Urban Gardening

Conclusion

Appendices

Book I: Foundations of Urban Gardening

Introduction

Urban soil, often overlooked amidst the steel and concrete of city landscapes, holds untold potential for transformation, growth, and connection. This chapter delves into the heart of urban gardening by unlocking the secrets of the soil beneath our feet, exploring its challenges, and presenting solutions to rejuvenate and harness its potential for green spaces in urban environments.

Urban soil is a complex tapestry woven from the past and present, reflecting the history of the land and the human activity that has shaped it. It tells stories of neglect and misuse, but also of resilience and renewal. Analysing and enhancing urban soil quality is not just a gardening task; it's an act of environmental stewardship, a commitment to sustainable living, and a step towards rekindling our connection with the natural world.

The journey of understanding urban soil begins with an exploration of its composition and the unique challenges it presents. From compaction and contamination to nutrient deficiencies, urban soils require careful analysis and strategic intervention to transform them into fertile ground for urban gardens. This process is both a science and an art, requiring knowledge, patience, and creativity.

Soil preparation techniques for urban spaces are diverse and innovative, reflecting the ingenuity of urban gardeners who work within the constraints of limited space and resources. From raised beds and container gardens to rooftop and vertical gardening, these techniques demonstrate that fertile soil can be cultivated almost anywhere, transforming even the smallest spaces into lush, productive gardens.

At the heart of soil revitalization is composting, the transformation of organic waste into "black gold." This section highlights the importance of composting in urban gardening, exploring how it enriches the soil, supports plant health, and contributes to a sustainable urban ecosystem. Composting is more than just waste management; it's a fundamental process that closes the loop of organic life, turning the end of one cycle into the beginning of another. This chapter aims to guide, inspire, and empower urban gardeners to look beyond the concrete, to see the potential in urban soil, and to take action to create vibrant, green spaces in the city. By understanding and nurturing urban soil, we can grow not just plants, but communities, ecosystems, and connections to the earth and each other.

Book I: Foundations of Urban Gardening

I. Understanding Urban Soil

Analysing and Enhancing Urban Soil Quality

In the heart of our cities, beneath the bustling streets and towering skyscrapers, lies a foundation teeming with potential—urban soil. Often overlooked, this soil holds the secret to transforming gray expanses into green oases. But first, we must embark on a journey of discovery and renewal. Have you ever stopped to consider what lies beneath the concrete?

Picture this: Maria, an urban gardener in a sprawling metropolis, digs into the soil of her small rooftop garden. She uncovers not just earth, but the story of the land itself. This soil, compacted and neglected, speaks of its past burdens and present resilience. It's a common tale in our cities, yet one that carries a beacon of hope. Maria, like many before her, seeks to unlock this soil's potential. Her story, and countless others, guide us through the art and science of rejuvenating our urban landscapes.

Analysing urban soil is our first step. This isn't mere digging; it's an investigation. What secrets does your soil hold? Testing for pH levels, contaminants, and nutrient content might reveal surprises. Sometimes, these tests unveil challenges, like lead from old paint or compacted layers that suffocate roots. Yet, within every challenge lies opportunity.

Enhancing soil quality is where creativity shines. It's akin to cooking; each addition must be thoughtful. Organic matter, like compost, acts as the soil's soul food, enriching it for future growth. Imagine transforming your kitchen scraps into the life force for your garden. This process is not just ecological; it's deeply personal, connecting us to the cycle of life.

In urban environments, space is a luxury. Yet, gardeners find innovative ways to prepare their soil. Raised beds, container gardens, and even old bathtubs become sanctuaries for plant life. Each solution is a testament to human ingenuity, proving that nature can thrive in the smallest of spaces.

Now, think about your own urban soil. What stories does it tell, and how can you help it flourish? Remember, each patch of earth, no matter how small, is a step towards greener, more vibrant cities. Let's embrace this journey together, transforming urban soil from overlooked to celebrated. Through analysis, enhancement, and preparation, we can turn even the most neglected spaces into thriving gardens. Are you ready to unlock the potential beneath your feet?

Soil Preparation Techniques for Urban Spaces

Have you ever wondered how a barren rooftop or a compacted backyard in the city could transform into a lush garden? The secret lies not in the seeds we sow but in how we prepare the urban soil that nurtures them. This journey of preparation is filled with innovation, community, and the promise of greenery amidst the concrete.

Let's take a moment to delve into the story of Alex, a dedicated urban gardener who turned a small, shaded corner of their apartment complex into a vibrant community garden. Faced with hard, nutrient-poor soil, Alex didn't see a dead end but a challenge to embrace. Their journey underscores a vital lesson: With the right techniques, even the most unyielding urban soil can become a cradle for growth.

First steps in soil preparation often involve breaking new ground—literally. But in an urban setting, it's not just about tilling the soil; it's about reimagining what soil can be. Alex and their neighbour's brought in fresh, organic topsoil, mixing it with local compost. Together, they layered these atop the existing ground, creating raised beds that would bypass the poor soil beneath. Have you considered how raised beds could transform your gardening experience?

But soil preparation doesn't stop with creating new planting areas. It's also about nurturing the soil. Alex introduced a regimen of composting, adding rich, organic matter to the beds. This practice didn't just improve soil structure; it fostered a deeper connection between the gardeners and the cycle of life and decay. They saw kitchen scraps not as waste but as the future lifeblood of their garden.

In these urban spaces, water is a precious resource. The community garden implemented a drip irrigation system, ensuring that every drop of water went straight to the roots of their plants. This method not only conserved water but also prevented the evaporation and runoff common in more traditional watering methods. Could drip irrigation be the solution your urban garden has been searching for?

Alex's story is one of many in the world of urban gardening, a testament to the creativity and resilience of city dwellers. Their garden became more than just a source of fresh produce; it was a haven for biodiversity, a place of learning, and a centre of community.

So, as we explore the myriad of soil preparation techniques available to urban gardeners, let's draw inspiration from these stories. From the practicality of raised beds and containers to the sustainability of composting and efficient water use, the possibilities are as varied as the gardeners themselves. What will your contribution to this growing tapestry be? Are you ready to roll up your sleeves and transform your piece of the urban landscape?

Composting: Black Gold for Urban Gardens

Imagine, if you will, a simple banana peel. In the hustle of urban life, it might find its end in a trash bin, destined for a landfill. Yet, what if this humble peel could be the key to revitalizing your garden's soil, transforming it into a rich, fertile foundation for your plants? This is the magic of composting, a process turning everyday waste into precious "black gold" for urban gardens.

Now, let me tell you about Jordan, a city dweller with a passion for sustainable living. Jordan's small balcony garden was struggling; the plants were weak, and the flowers were sparse. The turning point? Embracing composting. Jordan started with a simple worm bin, feeding it scraps from the kitchen. Over time, these scraps transformed into nutrient-rich compost, full of life and potential. When Jordan mixed this compost into the garden's soil, the transformation was remarkable. Plants thrived, flowers bloomed, and a once-struggling garden became a vibrant ecosystem. This story is a testament to the power of composting, a journey of transformation that begins with the most ordinary materials. But how does one start this journey in the cramped quarters of the urban jungle? It's simpler than you might think. Composting doesn't require a sprawling backyard. A bin in a kitchen corner, a worm composter under a sink, or a community composting program can all be beginnings. What matters is the action, the decision to start. Have you thought about where a compost bin could fit in your space?

The essence of composting lies not just in the end product but in the process— the daily contribution of scraps, the turning of the pile, the patience. It's a commitment to nurturing not just a garden but the environment at large. By diverting waste from landfills, reducing methane emissions, and returning nutrients to the soil, composting embodies the principles of sustainability and regenerative living.

Yet, composting is more than an environmental act; it's a story of connection. Through composting, urban gardeners like Jordan weave themselves into the cycle of life, turning waste into wealth, and in doing so, reconnect with the earth. This connection, rooted in the act of composting, blossoms into a broader awareness of our impact on the planet and the steps we can take toward a more sustainable future.

So, I invite you to consider: Could composting be the next step in your gardening journey? Whether you're a seasoned urban gardener or just beginning to explore the possibilities of your balcony or rooftop, composting offers a path to deeper engagement with your environment. It's a step towards transforming not just your garden, but your relationship with the natural world.

In the end, composting in urban gardens is a symbol of hope and resilience. It reminds us that, even in the concrete confines of the city, cycles of growth and renewal persist. The "black gold" produced in our compost bins is a testament to the potential for transformation that lies within and around us, waiting to be unlocked. Are you ready to turn your kitchen scraps into the foundation of a thriving urban oasis?

Conclusion

As we close this chapter on understanding urban soil, we reflect on the journey from viewing soil merely as a backdrop for urban life to recognizing it as a vital, living entity that sustains and enriches our environment. The exploration of urban soil analysis, enhancement, and preparation techniques has revealed the transformative power of gardening in the urban context, not only for the soil itself but for the gardeners and communities it nurtures.

The process of rejuvenating urban soil is emblematic of the broader challenges and opportunities of urban living. It requires us to confront and mitigate the impacts of pollution, compaction, and neglect while embracing innovative solutions to create sustainable, productive green spaces. This journey underscores the resilience of nature and the potential for renewal in even the most degraded soils, reminding us that with care, knowledge, and effort, growth and greenery can flourish amidst the concrete.

Composting, as the cornerstone of soil revitalization, emerges not just as a technique for waste management but as a philosophy of circular living, emphasizing renewal, sustainability, and connection to the natural cycles of life. This "black gold" epitomizes the essence of urban gardening: transforming the discarded into the treasured, fostering life in unexpected places, and weaving the fabric of a more sustainable urban ecosystem.

The exploration of urban soil is more than a gardening endeavour; it is a call to action for urban dwellers to engage with their environment, to transform their relationship with the land, and to participate in the creation of more green, vibrant, and sustainable cities. By understanding and nurturing urban soil, we plant the seeds for a future where urban spaces are not just livable but are alive with the buzz of bees, the flourish of foliage, and the bounty of harvests.

In cultivating urban soil, we cultivate hope, resilience, and connection. We learn that every small patch of earth holds the potential for change, growth, and renewal. This chapter is not just a guide to gardening but a manifesto for urban environmental stewardship, advocating for a world where the soil beneath our feet is recognized as the foundation for a healthier, greener, and more sustainable urban future.

Choosing Your Crops Wisely

Introduction

Embarking on the journey of urban gardening is akin to painting a masterpiece on a canvas of concrete and steel. It's a process filled with challenges and rewards, requiring a deep understanding of one's environment and the boldness to experiment. The choice of crops is not merely a matter of what one wishes to grow but a critical decision that shapes the garden's success. This chapter, "Choosing Your Crops Wisely," delves into the nuanced art of selecting the right plants for urban gardens, aiming to guide, inspire, and empower urban gardeners.

Urban environments present a unique set of challenges for gardening: limited space, varying degrees of sunlight, and the ever-present concrete that seems to stifle the natural world. Yet, within these constraints lies immense potential for creativity and growth. The urban gardener must become a connoisseur of their environment, understanding the subtle interplay of light, shadow, and seasons to create a thriving garden.

Selecting crops for urban gardens goes beyond mere preference or taste; it's about understanding the specific needs of each plant and how they align with the urban microclimate. It involves seasonal planning to ensure a year-round harvest, navigating the complexities of growing cycles, and making the most of limited space. Moreover, the cultivation of specialty crops introduces an element of biodiversity and cultural heritage, turning urban gardens into havens of rare and heirloom varieties that defy the homogeneity of commercial agriculture.

Yet, the journey of selecting crops is also a communal experience, weaving together the stories, experiences, and knowledge of urban gardeners. It's a journey that fosters community, encourages sustainability, and contributes to the larger narrative of urban resilience and environmental stewardship.

As we explore the intricacies of choosing crops wisely, we invite urban gardeners to embark on this journey with curiosity and courage. It's an adventure that promises not only the joy of harvest but also a deeper connection to the cycles of nature and the community of fellow gardeners. Through careful planning, creativity, and collaboration, urban gardens can become oases of biodiversity, sustainability, and beauty in the heart of the city.

Selecting Crops for Urban Environments

In the heart of the city, where the buzz of life never ceases, and the concrete jungle looms large, lies an oasis waiting to be born. Urban gardens, in their myriad forms, emerge as vibrant testaments to nature's resilience and human creativity. But have you ever wondered, amidst this bustling urban setting, which crops can transform a mere balcony or rooftop into a verdant paradise?

The journey into urban gardening begins with a crucial decision: selecting the right crops. This choice, far from arbitrary, sets the stage for the garden's success or struggles. So, how does one navigate this crucial step? Let's delve into the art and science of choosing crops wisely, guided by the experiences of those who've turned their urban constraints into lush, productive gardens. First, consider the unique canvas your city environment provides. Sunlight, often a coveted commodity in densely built areas, varies dramatically from one space to another. Have you noticed how certain corners of your potential garden catch the morning light, while others remain shrouded in shade? This observation is your first clue in selecting crops. Tomatoes and peppers bask in full sunlight, thriving where they can soak up those rays. Meanwhile, leafy greens like spinach and kale are more forgiving, able to flourish in partial shade.

Now, let's ponder the seasons. The urban landscape, with its concrete and asphalt, often defies the traditional rules of climate, creating microclimates that can extend growing seasons or provide refuge from early frosts. Have you experienced the surprise of warm pockets in your garden space during the colder months? This anomaly presents an opportunity to experiment with seasonal planning, choosing crops that leverage these unique urban conditions for a year-round harvest.

consider Tom's story. Living in a high-rise with just a small balcony for his garden, he discovered that his south-facing outdoor space received an ample amount of sunlight, even in the late autumn. Inspired, Tom planted a variety of herbs and leafy greens, and to his delight, found that his mini-garden provided fresh ingredients well beyond the expected growing season. Tom's experience underscores the importance of observation and adaptation in urban gardening. It's about using what you have to its fullest potential.

diversity in crop selection not only enriches the garden's yield but also its aesthetic and ecological balance. Have you thought about the array of colours, textures, and heights at your disposal? From the towering grace of okra plants to the vibrant hues of Swiss chard, your garden can become a canvas of biodiversity. This variety isn't just pleasing to the eye; it encourages a healthy ecosystem, attracting pollinators and beneficial insects that keep harmful pests at bay.

Transitioning to the topic of community, urban gardening often isn't a solitary endeavour. Do you recall a time when a fellow gardener shared a prized seedling or a tip that transformed your garden? These exchanges are the lifeblood of urban gardening communities. They enrich our gardens and our experiences, weaving individual efforts into a tapestry of collective achievement. Specialty crops, in particular, thrive in this environment of sharing and experimentation. They allow gardeners to explore unique flavours and traditions, contributing to the garden's diversity and the community's cultural richness.

Finally, the journey of selecting crops is an ongoing cycle of learning and growth. Each season offers lessons in success and failure, each plant a story of resilience or vulnerability. As urban gardeners, we become students of nature, constantly adapting and evolving our practices to meet the challenges and opportunities of our environment.

Choosing crops for an urban garden is an adventure in creativity, resilience, and community. It's a process that demands our attention and rewards us with beauty, sustenance, and connection. As we close this section, remember that the most successful gardens are those that reflect the unique conditions and spirit of their urban landscape. They are gardens born of careful observation, vibrant diversity, and a willingness to experiment and share.

Seasonal Planning for Year-Round Harvest

Embarking on the journey of urban gardening requires not just enthusiasm but a strategic approach to what you plant and when. The cycle of seasons, each with its own character and challenge, offers a canvas for the urban gardener. But how does one navigate this ever-changing landscape to ensure a bounty throughout the year?

Urban environments create unique microclimates. Have you noticed how certain areas in your garden space might retain warmth well into the cooler months? This phenomenon can extend your growing season. By carefully observing and noting these patterns, you can tailor your planting schedule to harness these microclimates, selecting crops that will thrive in them.

Winter, often seen as a dormant period, is anything but idle for the urban gardener. It's a time for reflection, learning from the past season's successes and setbacks. But, have you considered winter as a time for growth? With the right crops and techniques, such as cold frames or greenhouse planting, you can grow hearty greens even in the coldest months. Sharing a story, let's take inspiration from Lucia, who successfully harvested kale and spinach throughout winter, using nothing more than a small, homemade greenhouse on her balcony.

As the chill of winter recedes, spring offers a new beginning. This is the time to start seeds indoors for crops that require a longer growing season. Have you experienced the joy of seeing the first seedlings push through the soil? There's hardly a more rewarding sight for a gardener. But spring planting isn't without its risks—late frosts can threaten young plants. Here, using cloches or row covers as protection can be invaluable, a lesson learned the hard way by many urban gardeners, myself included.

Summer, with its abundant sunlight and warmth, is the season most associated with gardening. It's when tomatoes, peppers, and cucumbers flourish. However, managing water becomes crucial. Have you ever struggled with watering during the hot summer months? Drip irrigation systems and mulching can conserve moisture and keep your plants hydrated. An anecdote here involves a community garden that implemented a simple, yet effective, rainwater harvesting system, significantly reducing their water usage and fostering a sense of sustainability within the community. As summer wanes, autumn heralds a time of harvest and preparation for the coming colder months. But did you know that autumn is also perfect for planting crops that can overwinter? Garlic, onions, and some varieties of leafy greens can be planted now for an early spring harvest. Reflecting on a year's cycle, Ethan, an avid urban gardener, shares how a well-planned autumn garden provided him with a bountiful harvest of root vegetables and hardy greens, long after the first frost.

Achieving a year-round harvest in an urban environment often requires thinking outside the traditional gardening box. Vertical gardening, hydroponics, and indoor gardening under grow lights are just some methods that urban gardeners have adopted. Have you explored these innovative gardening techniques? Their potential to transform small spaces into productive gardens is nothing short of revolutionary.

Seasonal planning for urban gardening is a continuous cycle of observation, action, and reflection. Each year brings new lessons and opportunities to refine your approach, making your garden more resilient and productive. By embracing the rhythm of the seasons and integrating innovative gardening practices, you can enjoy the fruits (and vegetables) of your labor all year round.

Specialty Crops for Urban Gardeners

Have you ever marvelled at the resilience and versatility of urban gardens? Amidst the concrete landscape, these green spaces not only thrive but also tell a story of innovation, heritage, and community. In this journey through the world of specialty crops, we'll explore how unique, lesser-known plants can transform urban gardening spaces into rich, biodiverse ecosystems. But what makes a crop "specialty," and why should urban gardeners take notice?

Specialty crops stand out for their unique flavours, textures, and nutritional profiles. They often include heirloom varieties, exotic fruits, and herbs that are not typically found in conventional markets. But have you considered the role these crops play in biodiversity and cultural preservation? Take, for instance, the story of Maria, an urban gardener who cultivates rare, heirloom tomato varieties in her rooftop garden. Each tomato not only brings a burst of flavour but also carries the legacy of generations, a living link to her Italian heritage. Selecting the right specialty crops for your urban garden requires understanding your garden's microclimate and soil conditions. But how do you know which plants will thrive in your space? Experimentation is key. Remember Tom, who transformed his small balcony into a vibrant display of exotic herbs and edible flowers? His secret was starting small, experimenting with different plants to see what worked best in his limited space and adjusting his selections based on the results. When planning your garden, how do your account for the changing seasons? Seasonal planning is crucial, especially for specialty crops that may have specific growing requirements. Consider the story of Lena, who meticulously plans her garden so that spring's edible flowers make way for summer's exotic leafy greens, followed by autumn's heirloom squashes. Her garden is a testament to careful planning and the joy of harvesting a diverse array of crops year-round.

Cultivating specialty crops in urban settings presents unique challenges. Space limitations, variable sunlight, and the urban heat island effect can impact growth. Yet, urban gardeners find innovative solutions. Vertical gardening, container gardening, and the use of greenhouses are just a few methods employed to overcome these obstacles. Do you remember the community garden that installed a rooftop greenhouse? It became a year-round oasis of specialty greens and herbs, demonstrating the potential of collective effort and innovative thinking.

At the heart of urban gardening lies a strong sense of community. Specialty crops often become a medium for sharing knowledge, seeds, and harvests. Have you ever participated in a seed swap or tasted a dish made from a neighbor's garden produce? These experiences underscore the value of community in urban gardening, fostering connections and enriching our understanding of the world's diverse flora.

Choosing to grow specialty crops can have a profound impact on sustainability and urban biodiversity. These crops often require fewer resources and adapt well to organic growing methods, reducing the need for chemical inputs. Moreover, by cultivating plant diversity, urban gardens become havens for pollinators and beneficial insects, contributing to the health of the urban ecosystem. Have you considered the broader environmental impact of your garden's biodiversity?

The journey of growing specialty crops is one of continuous learning and adaptation. Successes and failures provide valuable lessons, shaping our approach to urban gardening. Reflecting on the stories shared, from Maria's heirloom tomatoes to the community's rooftop greenhouse, we see a common theme of resilience and innovation. What will your contribution to this ongoing story be?

Conclusion

As we conclude our exploration of "Choosing Your Crops Wisely," it's clear that the act of selecting crops for an urban garden is far more than a gardening task; it's a statement of intention and a step toward sustainable urban living. This chapter has traversed the complexities of urban gardening, from understanding microclimates and seasonal planning to the cultivation of specialty crops and fostering community connections. It has been a guide, a source of inspiration, and a call to action for urban gardeners to embrace the challenges and opportunities of their unique environments.

Urban gardening, with its constraints and possibilities, mirrors the broader challenges of urban living. It demands creativity, resilience, and an adaptive spirit. Yet, it also offers immense rewards: the satisfaction of a harvest, the beauty of green space in the concrete jungle, and the cultivation of community. The selection of crops becomes a critical pivot around which these experiences turn, influencing not only the success of the garden but also its impact on the gardener's life and the larger urban ecosystem.

The journey doesn't end with a successful harvest. It's a cyclical process of learning, growing, and sharing. Urban gardeners are encouraged to experiment with new varieties, share their successes and failures with their community, and continue to refine their approach to crop selection. Through this ongoing process, urban gardens can flourish, becoming more productive, diverse, and resilient.

Looking forward, the practice of wisely choosing crops for urban environments stands as a beacon of hope and sustainability. It exemplifies how, even in the most unlikely places, we can forge a connection with nature, contribute to biodiversity, and build resilient communities. Urban gardens are not just spaces for growing food; they are platforms for education, conservation, and social connection. They are small but significant counterpoints to the narrative of urban sprawl, offering a glimpse of a more sustainable, interconnected urban future.

In closing, "Choosing Your Crops Wisely" is more than a chapter in a gardening guide; it's an invitation to embark on a transformative journey. It's a journey that challenges urban gardeners to think creatively, act sustainably, and grow communally. As urban landscapes continue to evolve, the principles and practices outlined in this chapter will remain vital tools for those seeking to cultivate green spaces that nourish, inspire, and thrive.

Book II: Advanced Techniques for Urban Yield

Introduction

Start with the visual contrast between traditional gardening spaces and the modern urban landscape, highlighting the limited green spaces within cities. Pose a rhetorical question to engage the reader: "In a world dominated by concrete and steel, how can we reclaim our innate connection to the earth and foster green spaces where they're most needed?"

Briefly trace the evolution of gardening from rural to urban settings, emphasizing the shift in techniques necessitated by space constraints.

Mention the growing importance of sustainability and self-sufficiency in urban environments.

Introduce the concept of innovative planting techniques as solutions to the challenges of urban gardening, focusing on space-saving solutions, succession planting, intercropping strategies, and rooftop gardening essentials.

Use a transition phrase to smoothly link the historical context to the present-day relevance of these techniques.

Delve into the essence of each highlighted technique, briefly explaining its significance and potential impact on urban gardening.

Incorporate a short anecdote or personal story to illustrate the transformative power of innovative planting techniques in an urban setting.

Directly address the reader with questions about their experiences or aspirations regarding urban gardening, fostering a conversational tone.

Present the chapter as a guide not just to gardening but to reimagining urban spaces as areas of growth and sustainability.

Conclude the introduction with a forward-looking statement about the potential of innovative planting techniques to revolutionize urban gardening and by extension, urban living.

Transition smoothly into the main content of the chapter with an invitation to explore these techniques in detail.

Use varied sentence structures to maintain a dynamic and engaging rhythm throughout the introduction.

Ensure transitions between topics are smooth and logical, guiding the reader through your narrative seamlessly.

Keep the voice active to enhance clarity and directness.

Innovative Planting Techniques

Space-Saving Solutions: Vertical and Container Gardening

In the vast expanse of urban landscapes, where concrete often overshadows green, innovative planting techniques emerge as beacons of hope and sustainability. These methods are not just about gardening; they're about reclaiming space, fostering biodiversity, and creating sustainable ecosystems within our cities. But how do we navigate these techniques to maximize our green spaces effectively?

Have you ever looked at a bare wall or a small balcony and imagined it teeming with green life? Vertical and container gardening are transforming these underused spaces into lush, productive areas. Through the clever use of hanging planters, wall-mounted pots, and modular systems, urban gardeners are stacking upwards, defying the spatial limitations of city living.

But what does it take to create a successful vertical garden? Beyond aesthetics, it's about understanding the specific needs of plants in these unique conditions—considering factors like sunlight, water drainage, and weight. Imagine Sarah's balcony in downtown, where a mix of vertical planters and containers hosts everything from herbs to strawberries, creating not just a garden but a haven.

Transitioning smoothly, let's delve into succession planting and intercropping—techniques that promise a continuous harvest and a vibrant tapestry of plants. Succession planting involves staggering plantings weeks or months apart to ensure a constant supply of produce. Have you tried planting lettuce every two weeks to enjoy fresh greens throughout the season?

Intercropping, on the other hand, is about growing complementary plants together. This method can save space and even deter pests naturally. Picture John's small garden plot, where he plants onions between his carrots to repel carrot flies—a simple yet effective strategy that underscores the harmony possible within our ecosystems.

s we shift our gaze upwards, rooftop gardening presents a frontier for urban green spaces. But what does it take to transform a barren rooftop into a flourishing garden? Beyond the logistical challenges of weight and waterproofing, rooftop gardens offer a unique microclimate that can extend growing seasons and provide a sanctuary for pollinators amidst the urban sprawl.

Drawing inspiration from Lisa's rooftop oasis, we see how container gardening, raised beds, and even greenhouses can create micro-environments suitable for a wide range of crops. Her rooftop not only supplies her family with fresh vegetables but also serves as a community gathering space, demonstrating the potential of these gardens to foster social connections.

Throughout these explorations, personal stories bring to life the principles and practices of innovative planting techniques. These narratives not only offer practical insights but also inspire us to view our urban environments through a lens of potential and possibility. From Sarah's balcony garden to John's intercropped plot and Lisa's rooftop haven, each story highlights the adaptability and creativity inherent in urban gardening.

Innovative planting techniques offer more than just methods for gardening in limited spaces; they represent a paradigm shift in how we view our urban environments. They challenge us to see not just what is, but what could be—a city where every rooftop, balcony, and wall bursts with green life, contributing to biodiversity, food security, and the well-being of its inhabitants.

As we close this exploration, consider how you might apply these techniques in your own urban space. Whether it's starting a container garden on your windowsill, experimenting with intercropping in your backyard, or advocating for a community rooftop garden, each action is a step towards a greener, more sustainable urban future. What will your contribution be?

Succession Planting and Intercropping Strategies

Embarking on a journey through the realm of urban gardening introduces us to a world where innovation meets tradition, where the wisdom of centuries and the challenges of modern living intertwine. In this exploration, two pivotal techniques emerge as cornerstones for maximizing yield, diversifying crops, and ensuring a harmonious and productive garden: succession planting and intercropping. But how do these strategies come to life in the compact spaces of our urban landscapes?

Succession planting, a method as rhythmic as the seasons themselves, involves planting crops in sequences to ensure a continuous harvest. Have you ever marvelled at a garden that seems to offer new bounties with each visit? This is succession planting at work. It's about understanding the lifecycle of each plant and planning your garden so that as one crop matures, another begins to flourish.

Imagine your garden as a stage. In spring, the early act features leafy greens and radishes, swiftly followed by the vibrant performance of summer squash and beans. As the season

wanes, autumn brings a final, hearty display of kale and Brussels sprouts. This ongoing cycle not only maximizes the use of space but also keeps the soil actively engaged, reducing the risk of erosion and nutrient depletion.

intercropping, on the other hand, is the art of planting complementary crops together, creating a symphony of growth that utilizes space efficiently and fosters a balanced ecosystem. But what does this look like in practice? Picture a garden where tall sunflowers tower above, providing shade and support to climbing beans, while below, the soil is carpeted with fragrant herbs and sprawling squash. This is not just a method of planting; it's a model of coexistence and mutual benefit.

The success of intercropping lies in understanding the unique needs and characteristics of each plant, allowing them to complement rather than compete with one another. It's about recognizing that in diversity, there is strength—be it in pest management, soil health, or pollination. Each plant plays a role, contributing to the garden's overall health and productivity.

Delving into the personal experiences of urban gardeners brings these concepts to life. Take, for example, the story of Alex, who transformed a small rooftop into a lush oasis. Through succession planting,

Alex enjoys a varied harvest throughout the year, from spring's tender lettuces to winter's crisp cabbages. Meanwhile, Jamie's balcony garden, a marvel of intercropping, demonstrates how diverse plants can thrive together in limited space, with tomatoes, basil, and marigolds forming a vibrant, productive trio.

These stories not only inspire but also illustrate the practical applications of succession planting and intercropping in urban settings. They show us that with creativity, planning, and a willingness to experiment, even the smallest spaces can yield an abundance of fresh produce.

Embracing these innovative planting techniques does not come without its challenges. From selecting compatible plant pairs for intercropping to timing the planting sequences correctly in succession planting, urban gardeners must navigate a learning curve. Yet, it is within these challenges that the true joy of gardening unfolds.

As we reflect on the journey of integrating succession planting and intercropping into urban gardening practices, it becomes clear that these techniques are more than just strategies for maximizing yield—they are expressions of hope, resilience, and a commitment to sustainable living. They invite us to view our gardens as ecosystems, where each plant, each decision, contributes to a larger purpose.

So, what will your garden story be? How will you weave the principles of succession planting and intercropping into your urban oasis? The possibilities are as diverse and plentiful as the crops we choose to nurture.

Rooftop Gardening Essentials

In the heart of the city, where the sky meets the concrete, rooftop gardens emerge as sanctuaries of greenery, defying the urban sprawl. These spaces, often overlooked, hold the potential for not just beauty and tranquillity but also sustainability and community. But what does it take to transform a barren rooftop into a thriving garden? Let's embark on a journey through the essentials of rooftop gardening, where challenges turn into opportunities, and every square foot tells a story of innovation and resilience.

Have you ever gazed out over your city's rooftops and imagined them transformed into vibrant gardens? The vision of rooftop gardening is compelling, offering a glimpse into a future where urban spaces are not just liveable but alive. Yet, the path to realizing this vision is fraught with challenges. Weight restrictions, water management, and exposure to the elements are just a few hurdles that rooftop gardeners must navigate. How, then, do we turn these challenges into stepping stones towards creating lush, productive gardens in the sky?

Every successful garden begins with careful planning, and rooftop gardens are no exception. Assessing the structural integrity of the roof is paramount—can it support the weight of soil, plants, and water? Consulting with a structural engineer might be your first step. But have you also considered the accessibility of your rooftop? How will materials be transported up there, and how will water be supplied?

These logistical considerations lay the groundwork for a thriving rooftop garden.

With limited space and depth, selecting the right containers and soil becomes an art. Have you thought about the advantages of raised beds, which can offer ample growing depth while ensuring good drainage? Or perhaps modular planting systems that maximize space and minimize weight? The choice of soil is equally important. A lightweight, nutrient-rich mix can support plant health without overburdening the roof structure. Integrating personal stories, like that of Ava, who ingeniously used recycled materials to create raised beds, can illuminate the creative possibilities that rooftop gardening presents. Not all plants are suited to the unique conditions of a rooftop garden. Exposure to wind and sun, for instance, can be much more intense than at ground level. Have you considered how these factors will influence your plant selection? Hardy, drought-resistant plants often fare better, as do varieties that thrive in containers. From vibrant flowers to lush vegetables, the choice of plants can turn a rooftop into a haven for biodiversity. Sharing anecdotes, like Leo's rooftop orchard, underscores the potential for variety and abundance in rooftop gardens. One of the biggest challenges of rooftop gardening is ensuring plants receive enough water. Traditional watering methods might not be feasible, so what are the alternatives? Drip irrigation systems, rainwater harvesting, and self-watering containers are innovative solutions that conserve water and reduce labour. The story of Maya's rooftop garden, which thrives on a self-sustaining watering system, could inspire others to consider eco-friendly irrigation options.

Rooftop gardens have the potential to be more than just individual projects; they can foster community and connectivity. Have you thought about how your garden could serve as a communal space, hosting events or educational workshops? Gardens like these not only produce food but also grow relationships and knowledge, weaving together the fabric of urban communities.

The journey of rooftop gardening is one of continuous learning and adaptation. Facing and overcoming obstacles is part of the process, each challenge an opportunity to innovate. From dealing with pests in a rooftop setting to managing extreme weather conditions, the solutions urban gardeners devise are as diverse as the gardens themselves. Integrating stories of overcoming these obstacles can highlight the resilience and creativity inherent in rooftop gardening.

As we conclude our exploration of rooftop gardening essentials, it's clear that these spaces represent a vital component of the urban green infrastructure. They're not just about growing plants; they're about cultivating a greener, more sustainable future. Rooftop gardens challenge us to rethink our relationship with urban spaces, transforming underused areas into productive, life-affirming landscapes. What will your rooftop garden contribute to this vision?

Conclusion

begin with a reflection on the journey through innovative planting techniques, emphasizing the newfound understanding and appreciation for urban gardening's potential.

Reiterate the challenges urban gardeners face and how the techniques discussed offer practical, creative solutions.

Recap a few key personal stories or anecdotes from the chapter that highlight the successful application of these techniques, underscoring the practical benefits and lessons learned.

Encourage the reader to think about how these stories resonate with their own gardening experiences or aspirations.

discuss the broader implications of adopting innovative planting techniques in urban areas, including environmental sustainability, community building, and mental health benefits.

Use transition phrases to connect individual actions (gardening techniques) to larger outcomes (sustainable urban living).

Issue a call to action, urging readers to apply the innovative planting techniques in their own urban gardening endeavors, regardless of their experience level.

Pose direct questions to the reader about what techniques they're inspired to try or what changes they envision for their urban spaces.

Paint a vivid picture of what urban environments could look like with widespread adoption of innovative planting techniques, from green rooftops to vertical gardens in every available space.

Highlight the role of individual and community efforts in achieving this vision.

Offer some final thoughts on the journey of urban gardening, framing it as an ongoing process of learning, experimentation, and growth.

Conclude with an inspirational quote or a powerful statement that leaves the reader motivated to engage with urban gardening and to view it as a key component of urban innovation and sustainability.

Throughout the conclusion, continue to vary sentence structure and use active voice for a lively and engaging read.

Incorporate smooth transitions to ensure the conclusion is cohesive and reinforces the chapter's main themes.

Personal anecdotes or hypothetical scenarios can help to ground abstract concepts and inspire the reader to action.

Introduction

Imagine a garden where lush vegetables and vibrant flowers thrive, all year round, without a speck of soil in sight. This garden isn't set in an expansive countryside; instead, it's perched atop urban roofs, nestled in small balconies, and flourishing indoors under grow lights. Welcome to the world of hydroponics, a soilless cultivation method revolutionizing our approach to gardening. This innovative technique, which delivers nutrients directly to plants through water, is redefining what it means to grow food and ornamental plants alike. It presents a solution to the modern gardener's challenges: limited space, poor soil quality, and water use. Hydroponics promises a future where fresh produce can be grown anywhere—be it a bustling city or a barren landscape. Hydroponics is not a novelty of the modern era but has roots that trace back to ancient civilizations. However, it's within the context of today's environmental challenges and urbanization that hydroponics finds its most significant application. It offers a sustainable, efficient alternative for food production, minimizing water usage and maximizing space. As we embark on this hydroponic journey, we'll explore the foundations of designing your first hydroponic system, the intricacies of managing nutrients and water, and the joys of harvesting popular vegetables without a speck of soil.

II. Hydroponics: The Soilless Wonder

- **Designing Your First Hydroponic System**

Embark on a journey into the world of hydroponic gardening, a realm where water works wonders, and soil is surplus to requirements. This innovative approach to gardening has transformed balconies, rooftops, and indoor spaces into verdant sanctuaries, defying traditional gardening constraints. But what exactly propels the allure of hydroponics, especially for urban dwellers craving greenery amidst concrete?

Diving into hydroponics begins with crafting your inaugural system—a venture that might seem daunting at first. However, the essence of hydroponics lies in its simplicity and efficiency. From the basic wick system to more complex setups like nutrient film technique (NFT) or deep water culture (DWC), the options are vast. But how do you decide which system best suits your space and ambitions? Consider the tale of Alex, whose small apartment balcony became a lush lettuce haven using a simple DIY DWC system. His story is not just one of successful gardening but also of personal discovery and innovation.

Transitioning smoothly, the choice of system impacts the subsequent steps in your hydroponic journey, particularly in managing nutrients and water—a pivotal aspect of hydroponic gardening.

The lifeblood of hydroponic systems lies in the nutrient solution, providing plants with the essential elements they need to thrive. But have you ever pondered the science behind these solutions? Balancing nutrients is more art than science, requiring keen observation and adjustment. Engaging with the experiences of seasoned hydroponic gardeners can shed light on common pitfalls and best practices. For instance, Mia's venture into hydroponics was nearly derailed by nutrient imbalances, yet through trial and error, she mastered the delicate dance of nutrient management, turning her herbs vibrant and flavourful.

Navigating the intricacies of water management in hydroponics also unveils the importance of pH and conductivity monitoring—key factors that can make or break your garden's success. But how do you keep these parameters in check, and what tools can help you maintain the perfect balance?

The true test of a hydroponic system's efficacy comes down to the harvest. Growing popular vegetables like tomatoes, peppers, and leafy greens hydroponically not only promises year-round bounty but also a gratifying gardening experience. Yet, each vegetable presents its unique challenges and rewards. Did you know that certain varieties of tomatoes are better suited to hydroponic cultivation than others? Delving into the stories of urban gardeners who've navigated these challenges offers invaluable insights. From Kevin's rooftop pepper paradise to Leah's indoor herb collection, the personal journeys of hydroponic gardeners illuminate the path for newcomers.

hydroponic gardening, much like traditional gardening, flourishes with community. Sharing knowledge, successes, and failures not only enriches the individual gardener's experience but also strengthens the broader hydroponic community. Workshops, online forums, and garden clubs play pivotal roles in this ecosystem, fostering a culture of support and shared learning. Have you considered reaching out to your local hydroponic community or joining a digital forum to share your journey?

s we reflect on the journey into hydroponic gardening, it becomes clear that this method offers more than just an alternative to traditional gardening; it represents a sustainable, efficient, and rewarding approach to cultivating food and beauty in urban spaces. The innovation inherent in hydroponic gardening challenges us to rethink our relationship with nature, encouraging a deeper engagement with the process of growth and sustenance.

In conclusion, stepping into hydroponic gardening opens up a world of possibilities. It's an invitation to innovate, learn, and connect with both the plants we nurture and the community of gardeners we join. The stories of Alex, Mia, Kevin, and Leah remind us that every hydroponic garden starts with a single step—a decision to try something new. So, what will your hydroponic journey look like, and how will you share it with the world?

Managing Nutrients and Water in Hydroponics

Embarking on the journey of hydroponic gardening introduces us to a world where precision meets productivity in an environment where meticulous management of nutrients and water leads to astonishing growth and yields. Understanding the balance necessary to ensure plants thrive in a hydroponic system is crucial. At the core of hydroponic gardening lies the nutrient solution, a carefully balanced concoction that serves as the lifeline for plants, providing them with all the necessary elements for growth directly to their roots. This process, while complex, becomes rewarding as one delves deeper into the needs of plants at various growth stages.

The quality of water, the medium carrying these vital nutrients, significantly impacts plant health. Monitoring parameters like pH levels and dissolved oxygen content can initially seem overwhelming. Yet, stories from the hydroponic community, such as Sam's experience revitalizing his garden by adjusting the water's pH, highlight the importance of water quality. The transition to practical strategies involves selecting the right nutrient formula tailored to each plant's specific dietary requirements, which can vary not only by species but also by growth phase. The integration of technology, including digital pH meters and EC testers, has simplified the monitoring and adjustment of nutrient and water parameters, making hydroponics more accessible to novices and turning apprehension into passion for gardeners like Emily. Despite the benefits, challenges in nutrient and water management are inevitable, ranging from imbalances in nutrient levels to water quality issues affecting plant health. However, each obstacle offers a lesson, enriching the gardener's understanding of their hydroponic system. The hydroponic gardening community plays a vital role in overcoming these challenges, offering a platform for sharing experiences and fostering a deeper understanding of managing nutrients and water effectively.

In conclusion, managing nutrients and water in hydroponics is both an art and a science, requiring diligence, patience, and a willingness to adapt. The journey towards mastering these aspects is filled with challenges, but the rewards of healthy, vibrant plants and bountiful harvests make it worthwhile. Engaging with the hydroponic community not only enhances this journey but also contributes to a richer, more fulfilling gardening experience. As you continue to explore hydroponic gardening, remember that each step taken towards mastering nutrient and water management not only brings you closer to a thriving garden but also deepens your connection to the process of growing food, inviting you to share your story and contribute to the ever-growing body of hydroponic gardening knowledge.

Growing Popular Vegetables Hydroponically

Embarking on the hydroponic journey opens up a world where the essence of growth isn't tethered to the traditional soil-bound roots but floats in nutrient-rich solutions, promising a future where food can flourish in the smallest of urban spaces. Have you ever paused to wonder at the simplicity and yet the profound efficiency of feeding plants directly through their water? This marvel is at the heart of hydroponic gardening, a method that not only conserves precious resources but also provides a bounty of fresh produce right at your doorstep.

Designing your first hydroponic system marks the beginning of an intimate dance with the intricacies of plant needs and water chemistry. Whether you opt for a simple Wick system or venture into the realms of NFT or DWC, the choice heralds a commitment to understanding the silent language of plants. Remember, every great invention began as a simple idea. Consider the story of Jamie, who, with a few PVC pipes and a pump from an old aquarium, built a system that grew lettuce so crisp it became the talk of her neighbourhood.

At the core of hydroponic success lies the alchemy of balancing nutrients and water—a potion that brings life to your garden. But how do you concoct this magical mixture? It's not merely about mixing water with nutrients; it's about understanding the delicate balance that different vegetables crave. Each plant has its tale, its unique thirst for certain minerals and conditions. Dive into the narrative of Max, who meticulously adjusted pH levels and nutrient concentrations, discovering the perfect recipe for his heirloom tomatoes that tasted of sunshine and earth, despite never touching soil. The choice of vegetables to grow hydroponically can paint your garden with a palette of flavours and colours. From the lush greens of spinach and kale to the vibrant reds of tomatoes and the deep purples of eggplants, each vegetable adds a stroke of beauty to your hydroponic canvas. But beyond aesthetics, have you pondered the satisfaction of harvesting your dinner mere steps from your kitchen? The joy of plucking a fresh pepper for your meal is unparalleled. Delve into the experiences of those who've walked this path, like Sarah, who transformed her small balcony into a cornucopia of herbs and vegetables, finding not just food but fulfillment in her hydroponic garden.

Hydroponic gardening, while rewarding, is not without its hurdles. Managing nutrient levels, ensuring adequate light, and combating pests in a soilless environment require patience and perseverance. Yet, each challenge is a stepping stone to mastery. Stories of resilience abound, like that of Leo, who battled root rot with research and innovation, emerging with a garden more resilient and productive than ever.

Hydroponic gardening is more than a method of cultivation; it's a symphony of growth, innovation, and community. It challenges us to reimagine our relationship with food and nature. As you embark on this journey, remember that each step forward is a part of a larger movement towards sustainability and self-sufficiency. Your hydroponic garden is a testament to what can be achieved when we harmonize with nature, even within the confines of our urban dwellings.

In embracing hydroponic gardening, you join a chorus of gardeners who've found in water a new soil, in nutrients a new sun, and in their harvests, a new connection to the earth. What will your hydroponic journey yield? How will the stories of Jamie, Max, Sarah, and Leo inspire your path, and how will you add your voice to this growing narrative of innovation and abundance?

Conclusion

Reflecting on our journey through "Hydroponics: The Soilless Wonder," we've traversed from the visionary potential of hydroponic gardening to the tangible rewards it offers. Hydroponic gardening is more than a method; it's a movement towards sustainable, resilient urban agriculture. It answers the call for water conservation, efficient space use, and the year-round production of fresh, nutritious produce. The path of hydroponic gardening, filled with learning and experimentation, challenges gardeners to become stewards of their miniature ecosystems, mastering the balance of nutrients and water to cultivate thriving plants.

The challenges faced along the way—be it mastering nutrient solutions or optimizing water conditions—are but stepping stones to a rewarding harvest. They teach patience, innovation, and the importance of community among gardeners. Looking ahead, the potential of hydroponics extends beyond individual gardens to global solutions for food security and sustainability. It envisions cities where rooftops and balconies are alive with greenery, contributing to a healthier planet.

As we conclude, let this exploration of hydroponics serve as an invitation to you, the reader, to venture into soilless gardening. Whether you're drawn to the sustainability aspect, the efficiency of water use, or the sheer joy of harvesting fresh produce from your living space, hydroponics offers a fulfilling path forward. It's a commitment to cultivating not just plants, but a sustainable future, one hydroponic system at a time. Embrace the journey, for the world of hydroponics is ripe with possibilities, ready to transform rooftops and balconies into verdant oases of life.

Introduction

Imagine the transformation of a small urban space into a lush garden where each plant thrives, pushing the boundaries of yield and health despite the concrete surroundings. This vision is at the heart of urban gardening, a pursuit that challenges and rewards in equal measure. Urban gardens are more than just collections of plants; they are testaments to the resilience and innovation of those who tend them. Within these green enclaves, the practices of natural fertilization, mindful watering, and strategic pruning and training emerge not just as tasks but as art forms—each technique a brushstroke in the gardener's palette, designed to enhance the vibrancy and productivity of the garden.

Yet, embarking on this journey of cultivation, especially within the unique confines of urban settings, requires more than just a will to grow; it requires knowledge, patience, and a willingness to learn and adapt. It's a path that leads gardeners through the complexities of nurturing plant life in less-than-ideal conditions, teaching them to coax abundance from limitation. This narrative unfolds with an exploration of natural fertilization strategies that feed the soil and soul, watering techniques that conserve precious resources while quenching plants' thirst, and methods of pruning and training that encourage growth and yield beyond expectations. These practices, however, are not just about the technicalities of gardening; they're about establishing a deeper connection with the environment. They prompt urban gardeners to question, experiment, and innovate, turning balconies, rooftops, and small patches of land into productive and sustainable oases. Through stories of success and lessons from failures, gardeners share a collective wisdom that enriches not only their gardens but also their lives and communities. This journey through the world of urban gardening is an invitation to embrace the challenges and joys of growing, to see potential in every small space, and to contribute to a greener, more sustainable urban landscape.

Optimizing Plant Health and Yield

Natural Fertilization Strategies

Embarking on the journey of urban gardening, where space is a premium and every leaf counts, requires a dive into innovative practices that promise not just survival but thriving vegetation. At the heart of this green quest lies the trinity of plant care: natural fertilization strategies, adept watering techniques, and the nuanced art of pruning and training. This narrative unfolds the tapestry of urban gardening, threading through the practices that turn concrete-bound dreams into lush realities.

In the realm of urban gardening, the introduction of natural fertilization strategies emerges as a cornerstone for plant health. Imagine transforming kitchen scraps into gold—compost gold, that is. This alchemy not only enriches the soil but also fosters a living microbiome, vital for plant growth. Stories abound of urban gardeners who, with the magic of compost, have turned their balconies into verdant escapes, underscoring the transformative power of natural fertilization. Yet, the journey doesn't stop at compost. Green manures and organic fertilizers also play pivotal roles, painting a broader stroke on the canvas of natural fertilization. It's a tale of return, where what comes from the earth generously gives back, completing a cycle that nurtures both plants and the planet.

As the narrative flows, the spotlight shifts to the lifeline of all gardens: water. The challenge of watering in the urban jungle, where every drop counts, calls for innovation. Techniques like drip irrigation and self-watering containers rise as champions, ensuring that plants receive their vital nourishment without waste. Yet, beyond the mechanics, lies the harmony of timing and quantity— knowing just when and how much to water. This knowledge often comes adorned with anecdotes, such as that of a gardener whose rooftop garden thrived against all odds, thanks to the prudent use of collected rainwater, illustrating that with creativity, even the scarce urban rain can turn into a plentiful harvest.

The narrative then delicately twines around the art of pruning and training plants. This is where the gardener, with a careful hand and an insightful eye, guides the plant in a dance of growth. Strategic cuts and supports not only shape the plant but also invigorate it, encouraging fruitful yields and deterring diseases. It's a practice steeped in attentiveness and patience, rewarding the gardener with the bounty of their toil. Through the lens of those who've mastered these techniques, we glean insights into maximizing productivity, whether it's through the judicious pruning of a tomato plant or the meticulous training of a vine along a sunny wall. Their successes underscore the essence of plant care—growth directed, not dictated.

Woven through this narrative of urban gardening are the threads of personal stories—tales of triumph, experimentation, and sometimes, failure. These anecdotes bring to life the abstract, making the techniques and strategies discussed not just information but shared experiences. Engaging directly with the reader, these stories pose questions, invite imagination, and offer a mirror to the reader's aspirations and challenges in gardening. It's through these reflections that the text transforms from a monologue into a conversation, from information to inspiration.

In conclusion, this journey through the trinity of urban gardening practices—natural fertilization, watering, and pruning—culminates in a vision of urban greenery that is both lush and sustainable. It's a testament to the ingenuity and resilience of urban gardeners who navigate the constraints of space and resources to create thriving gardens. As this chapter closes, the invitation to embark on this green journey remains open, reminding us that in the heart of the urban expanse, there lies the potential for verdant growth, for yield beyond measure, all waiting for the gardener's hand to awaken.

Watering Techniques for Urban Gardens

In the heart of the city, where green spaces are treasures hidden amongst concrete, the art of urban gardening flourishes, presenting a unique set of challenges and rewards. One critical aspect that stands at the forefront of cultivating a lush urban oasis is mastering the art of watering. How do urban gardeners ensure their plants receive just the right amount of water, a task made more complex by the confines and constraints of city living?

Watering techniques for urban gardens are not just about delivering water to plants; they're about doing so efficiently, sustainably, and effectively, ensuring that every drop contributes to plant health and yield. The urban gardener often turns to innovative solutions, balancing resource limitations with the needs of their thriving gardens. From simple setups to sophisticated systems, the approach to watering in the urban landscape is as varied as the gardens themselves.

One of the first strategies often explored is the use of self-watering containers. These ingenious systems, which allow plants to draw water as needed, are a testament to the innovation thriving in urban gardening communities. But have you considered the intricacies of setting up such a system, or the satisfaction of seeing your plants thrive, practically caring for themselves? Stories of success, like that of an urban gardener who transformed her balcony into a self-sustaining vegetable garden, inspire and illustrate the potential of such techniques.

Yet, the conversation on watering doesn't end with self-watering containers. Drip irrigation, a technique borrowed from large-scale agriculture, has found a place in the compact urban garden. Its precision and efficiency in delivering water directly to the roots of plants, minimizing waste and evaporation, make it a favoured choice. But implementing a drip system in the confined space of an urban garden requires creativity and adaptability—qualities in abundance among city dwellers turned gardeners.

Rainwater harvesting introduces another layer to the urban gardener's approach to watering. In cities, where every inch of green space counts, collecting rainwater to sustain gardens not only conserves precious resources but also connects gardeners more closely to the natural cycles of their environment. The journey from installing a simple barrel to integrating a fully functional rainwater irrigation system can be filled with challenges, yet it remains one of the most rewarding endeavours for the urban gardener. Through trial and error, the urban garden becomes not just a space of cultivation but a model of sustainability.

Amid these techniques, the principle of timing and moderation in watering remains paramount. Overwatering is as much a peril as under-watering, particularly in the varied environments of urban gardens, from shaded balconies to sun-drenched rooftops. The wisdom to navigate this balance often comes from experience, from paying close attention to the plants' cues, and from the shared knowledge within the gardening community. Engaging with fellow urban gardeners, whether through online forums, garden clubs, or local workshops, opens up a wellspring of advice and support, helping to refine watering techniques and strategies. In reflecting on the art of watering in urban gardens, it becomes clear that this aspect of gardening is about more than just plant care—it's about stewardship of the environment, about innovation in the face of limitations, and about the joy of nurturing growth in unexpected places. As urban gardeners master the techniques of efficient watering, they not only optimize the health and yield of their plants but also contribute to a larger movement towards sustainable living within the urban landscape.

In conclusion, the exploration of watering techniques for urban gardens reveals a landscape rich with innovation, challenge, and fulfillment. From the self-sufficiency of self-watering containers to the sustainability of rainwater harvesting and the precision of drip irrigation, these strategies embody the adaptability and resilience of urban gardeners. As we delve into the stories of those who have navigated the complexities of urban watering, we find not just guidance but inspiration. The urban garden, with all its constraints and possibilities, becomes a testament to what can be achieved when we approach our limitations with creativity and care.

Pruning and Training Plants for Maximum Productivity

Navigating the urban jungle, where space is a premium and greenery a cherished companion, the urban gardener embarks on a quest not merely to cultivate, but to elevate their garden to a beacon of productivity and health. This journey into the realms of pruning and training plants unveils a hidden dialogue between gardener and green, a silent conversation where each snip and support speak volumes about care, intention, and the pursuit of garden perfection.At the heart of this pursuit lies the nuanced art of pruning, a method less about mere trimming and more about thoughtful selection, about deciding which branches will form the foundation of a plant's future growth and productivity. It's a practice grounded in a deep understanding of plant biology, yet it's also an art form, painting potential with each precise cut. Through the lens of seasoned urban gardeners, we glimpse the transformative power of pruning. Their tales illuminate the path from novice clippers in hand to yielding shears with confidence, guiding plants towards abundant futures.

Coupled with pruning is the technique of training, an equally deliberate act of shaping the plant's physical structure to optimize its exposure to essential elements like sunlight and air. This practice, ranging from simple stakes that encourage upright growth to intricate trellis systems that support sprawling vines, reveals an architectural dimension to gardening. Training plants is akin to sculpting living greenery, with each support and tie contributing to the plant's ultimate form and productivity.

As we weave through the garden, transitioning from the why to the how, it becomes clear that these techniques are not just about enhancing yield. They are about overcoming the spatial challenges inherent in urban gardening, transforming balconies and rooftops into lush, efficient ecosystems. Questions naturally arise, prompting reflection and curiosity. How might one's garden transform with the application of these strategies? What untapped potential lies within each plant, waiting to be unlocked through careful pruning and strategic training?

The narrative rhythm shifts, balancing the concise, potent impact of short sentences against the detailed richness of longer explanations. This dynamic flow keeps the reader engaged, mirroring the varied pace of garden life—from the swift joy of a successful prune to the slow satisfaction of watching a trained vine flourish. Employing an active voice, the text becomes a direct conversation, a guide speaking clearly and confidently to the reader, offering advice, sharing insights, and celebrating the successes of fellow gardeners. This approach not only enhances clarity but also empowers the reader, encouraging them to take shears and ties into their hands and see their garden not as a static space but as a canvas for creativity and growth. Among these practical tips and techniques, personal stories of urban gardening successes and challenges weave a rich tapestry of experiences. These anecdotes bring abstract concepts to life, making the benefits of pruning and training tangible. They serve as beacons of inspiration, showcasing what is possible when dedication meets knowledge when a gardener's vision for their space meets the adaptable resilience of plant life.

In conclusion, the narrative culminates in a vision of what urban gardening can achieve when armed with the knowledge and tools for effective pruning and training. This exploration is not merely instructional but transformative, inviting urban gardeners to view their green spaces with new eyes, to see potential in every plant and possibility in every limited space. As the chapter closes, the invitation remains open: to experiment, to learn, and to grow—not just plants, but a deeper, more rewarding connection with the very act of gardening itself. In this dialogue between gardener and green, in the careful dance of pruning and training, lies the heart of urban garden productivity and health—a testament to the creativity and resilience that flourishes in the spaces between concrete and sky.

Conclusion

As the chapter on optimizing plant health and yield concludes, it's clear that the journey of urban gardening is both a personal and communal adventure. It's a path paved with the satisfaction of biting into a tomato warmed by the sun, of watching a bee buzz among city flowers, and of sharing the harvest with neighbors. The strategies and practices discussed—each a step towards more productive, healthy plants—are not endpoints but gateways to deeper understanding and connection with the cycle of life.

This narrative doesn't just end with the last period; it extends an invitation to continue exploring, learning, and growing. For the urban gardener, every day brings new challenges and opportunities, each plant a lesson in resilience, each harvest a reward for dedication and care. The stories woven through this text are but a few threads in the rich tapestry of urban gardening, each contributing to a larger picture of sustainability, community, and the sheer joy of watching things grow.

In embracing the principles of natural fertilization, efficient watering, and thoughtful pruning and training, urban gardeners do more than optimize plant health and yield; they sow the seeds for a future where green spaces flourish in the heart of the city. This future, vibrant and thriving, is not a distant dream but a growing reality, cultivated by the hands and hearts of gardeners who dare to see beyond the concrete—to envision a world where every urban space has the potential to bloom.

Book III: Ecological Pest and Disease Management

Introduction

Embark on an exploration into the heart of urban gardening, a vibrant testament to nature's resilience amidst the urban sprawl. Here, every leaf, flower, and fruit tell a story of triumph over adversity, a narrative punctuated by the gardener's ongoing battle against pests and diseases. But what if this story could be rewritten, not as a battle, but as a dance with nature? This chapter invites you on such a journey, offering knowledge as your compass and natural solutions as your guide.

Imagine standing in your urban garden, surrounded by the fruits of your labour, only to notice the subtle signs of an unwelcome visitor. How do you respond?

With curiosity, armed with the knowledge that every challenge in the garden is an opportunity to learn, to grow, and to adapt. Through engaging questions and vivid scenarios, we delve into the world of garden pests and diseases, transforming the urban gardener from a solitary sentinel into a savvy steward of their green space.

The stories shared within these pages, from the balcony gardener who outwitted aphids to the community plot that overcame blight, are not just tales of challenge and conquest. They are invitations to view our gardens as ecosystems, where balance, not battle, is the goal. These narratives, enriched with practical examples and enlivened with a dynamic mix of sentence structures and an active voice, guide us through the strategies that can protect and enhance our urban oases.

Understanding and Preventing Pests and Diseases

Common Pests in Urban Gardens and How to Identify Them

Dive headfirst into the vibrant world of urban gardening, a realm where lush greenery battles against the concrete backdrop of the city, and where every plant tells a story of resilience and growth. But lurking within these tales of urban greenery are less welcome narratives—those of the pests that threaten to undermine our horticultural efforts. How do we, as stewards of these urban oases, navigate the challenges posed by these tiny adversaries? Let's embark on a journey to uncover the secrets of identifying and managing common garden pests, transforming potential threats into chapters of success in our gardening stories.

Imagine, for a moment, you're inspecting your beloved garden when you spot something amiss on the underside of a leaf—a cluster of tiny, pear-shaped insects sucking the sap from your plants. What could these invaders be? Yes, they're aphids, one of the most common foes in the urban garden. But how do we tackle these sap-suckers without harming our green haven? This question leads us into the realm of natural pest control techniques, where the answers lie not in harsh chemicals, but in harmony with nature.

Through varied sentence structures and an engaging active voice, we'll explore the dynamics of urban garden ecosystems. Consider the caterpillar munching away at your cabbages—did you know that by introducing certain beneficial insects, you could naturally curb their appetite for your greens? Or that a simple homemade spray could deter a multitude of pests, safeguarding your garden's biodiversity?

Personal stories from the front lines of urban gardening bring these concepts to life. Picture Maria, who transformed her rooftop garden from a pest battleground to a thriving vegetable haven using nothing but neem oil and companion planting. Her tale is not just instructional; it's inspirational, showcasing the power of resilience and ingenuity in the face of urban gardening challenges.

As we weave through the narrative, smooth transitions guide us from one topic to the next, ensuring you're not just following along, but are immersed in the journey. From the unsettling realization of a pest problem to the satisfaction of implementing a successful natural solution, each step is a leap towards becoming more adept, informed gardeners.

In conclusion, our exploration of pests in the urban garden is more than a mere guide; it's an invitation to engage more deeply with the natural world right at our doorstep. Armed with the knowledge to identify common pests and the tools to manage them naturally, we're not just defending our plants; we're embracing an approach to gardening that's sustainable, effective, and, above all, respectful of the intricate web of life that thrives in our urban jungles.

Through direct questions, hypothetical scenarios, and the shared experiences of fellow gardeners, we've embarked on a narrative journey that's both enlightening and empowering. As you look back at your garden, now equipped with the insights and strategies to foster its health and productivity, consider this not the end, but a vibrant new chapter in your urban gardening adventure, where pests are but a bump in the road to a flourishing green space.

Natural Pest Control Techniques

Venture into the vibrant world of urban gardening, a realm where lush vegetation thrives amidst the hustle of city life, transforming balconies, rooftops, and backyards into verdant sanctuaries. Yet, this green idyll faces constant threats from an array of garden pests—unseen invaders that challenge the urban gardener's resolve and ingenuity. How, then, does one navigate these challenges, turning potential adversity into a testament to the resilience of nature and the human spirit?

Imagine discovering the first signs of aphid infestation on your cherished roses or spotting the telltale webbing of spider mites beneath the leaves of your tomatoes. What steps would you take to protect your urban oasis without resorting to harsh chemicals that harm more than just the pests they target? Herein lies the journey toward mastering natural pest control techniques—a path that intertwines respect for the environment with the practical needs of urban gardening.

Consider the introduction of beneficial predators, such as ladybugs and lacewings, into your garden. These natural allies embark on a relentless hunt for aphids and other pests, restoring balance without a drop of pesticide. But how do you attract these guardians to your garden? The answer often lies in the plants themselves—marigolds, lavender, and other fragrant herbs not only add beauty and aroma to your urban garden but also serve as beacons for beneficial insects.

Transitioning smoothly from predators to plants, another layer of defence emerges through the practice of companion planting. The strategic placement of certain plants side by side can create a natural barrier against pests, with some combinations even enhancing the growth and flavour of your garden produce. Have you ever planted garlic near your roses to fend off aphids, or paired basil with tomatoes for both its companionable properties and culinary delights?

The narrative of natural pest control is rich with personal stories and practical examples that bring abstract concepts to life. Picture John, an urban gardener who transformed his small balcony garden into a productive and pest-free zone using only organic methods. His success story, shared among the community, inspires others to explore the possibilities of natural pest control, demonstrating that even in the densest urban environments, nature offers solutions to those willing to observe, learn, and collaborate. As we delve deeper into the realm of natural pest management, engaging directly with the reader through questions and interactive scenarios, we uncover a dynamic and accessible narrative. The diverse sentence structures and active voice keep the text lively, enhancing readability and engagement. Each section flows seamlessly into the next, guiding the reader through the intricacies of urban pest management, from the challenges posed by common garden pests to the innovative strategies that urban gardeners employ to mitigate these threats.

In concluding this exploration of natural pest control techniques, we're reminded of the broader impact of our gardening choices. By opting for natural solutions, urban gardeners not only protect their plants but also contribute to the sustainability of their urban ecosystems. This narrative is not merely a guide but an invitation to embrace the challenges and joys of urban gardening, to experiment with natural pest control methods, and to share in the collective wisdom of a community committed to fostering green, productive spaces in the heart of the city.

Preventing Diseases in Dense Plantings

Step into the world of urban gardening, a place where the vibrant colours of nature defy the grey of concrete and steel. Here, amidst the serene beauty of blossoming spaces tucked between city buildings, a silent battle wages against invisible foes. Have you ever paused, trowel in hand, and wondered what secrets lie beneath the serene surface of your urban oasis? How do these hidden adversaries, the pests and diseases, find their way into our carefully cultivated spaces, and more importantly, how do we keep our green sanctuaries safe from their grasp?

Imagine, for a moment, your garden thriving under the gentle care of natural guardians. Picture ladybugs, those spotted sentinels, patrolling leaves for aphids, or the humble marigold, its bright blooms repelling nematodes with nothing but its presence. This isn't just a gardener's daydream; it's a practical approach to pest management that respects the delicate balance of urban ecosystems. But how do we begin to integrate these natural defenders into our garden strategy?

Consider the journey of Emma, a city dweller turned urban gardener, who transformed her rooftop space from a pest-ridden plot to a flourishing vegetable garden. Faced with an onslaught of aphids, she turned not to chemical sprays but to a squadron of ladybugs and a strategic planting of garlic and chives. Her story is a testament to the power of natural pest control methods, illustrating that even in the densest urban environments, nature offers solutions.

Transitioning seamlessly from pest control to disease prevention, we delve into the importance of maintaining plant health in densely packed urban gardens. Why do diseases spread more rapidly in these compact spaces, and what can be done to prevent them? It turns out that the key lies not in fighting nature, but in understanding it. By ensuring proper spacing, encouraging beneficial insects, and selecting disease-resistant plant varieties, we can create a garden environment that's not just resistant to pests and diseases but also thrives because of its biodiversity.

But what about watering, that most basic of gardening tasks? Here, too, lies an opportunity for innovation. Overhead watering in the cool of the evening might seem harmless, but did you know it can create conditions ripe for disease? By adopting drip irrigation and watering at the base of plants, we not only conserve water but also direct it where it's most needed, reducing the risk of fungal diseases.

The narrative of urban gardening is rich with stories like Emma's, each sharing valuable lessons on integrating natural pest and disease control into our gardening practices. These stories are not just instructions; they're inspirations, showing us that with a bit of knowledge and a lot of passion, we can turn our urban gardens into models of sustainability and resilience.

As we conclude this exploration into the vibrant world of urban gardening, we're reminded that the challenges we face—from pests to diseases—are but opportunities for growth. Armed with the knowledge of natural control techniques and inspired by the successes of fellow gardeners, we're not just growing plants; we're nurturing ecosystems. Our urban gardens, small though they may be, are part of a larger environmental tapestry, where every choice we make contributes to a healthier, greener planet.

Conclusion

As our journey through the challenges of pests and diseases in urban gardening concludes, we find ourselves at the threshold of a new understanding. No longer are these challenges seen as mere obstacles but as integral parts of the urban gardening experience, each offering lessons on resilience, balance, and the importance of natural stewardship.

The journey doesn't end here; it merely shifts towards a future where urban gardens are not just surviving but thriving, through the adoption of sustainable practices that work in harmony with nature. The stories of success we've shared illuminate the path forward, showcasing the power of community, the value of shared knowledge, and the transformative impact of adopting a holistic approach to garden care.

We're called to action, and encouraged to take the insights and strategies explored in this chapter and weave them into the fabric of our urban gardening practices. By doing so, we join a growing movement of gardeners who see beyond the confines of their plots to the larger picture of urban sustainability and ecological balance. Looking forward, the vision is clear: a world where urban gardens are vibrant ecosystems, where gardeners are guardians of biodiversity, and where pests and diseases are managed not with chemicals but with knowledge and care. This future is not just possible; it's within reach, waiting for us to take the next step in our gardening journey. Together, let's cultivate this future, growing more than plants—we're growing a green, resilient world, one urban garden at a time.

Introduction

In the heart of the urban jungle, amidst the concrete and steel, lie hidden oases of greenery that defy the urban sprawl, creating pockets of vibrant life. These urban gardens are not just spaces of beauty and growth but testaments to resilience and sustainability in the face of environmental challenges. "Building Resilience in Your Garden" is more than a guide; it's a journey into the heart of urban gardening, exploring how even the smallest spaces can transform into ecosystems brimming with life.

This chapter delves into the foundational practices that empower gardeners to foster gardens that are not only productive but also resilient. From encouraging beneficial insects and employing companion planting to understanding the intricate balance of urban ecosystems, the strategies outlined here are designed to guide you in creating a garden that thrives in harmony with nature.

As urban gardeners, our challenge is to see beyond the confines of our plots, to understand our gardens as living systems that interact with the environment around them. This understanding prompts us to adopt practices that support the health and productivity of these systems, ensuring they can withstand and adapt to the pressures of urban gardening. Whether you're a seasoned gardener or just beginning, this chapter offers insights into making your garden a bastion of resilience in the urban landscape.

Building Resilience in Your Garden

Encouraging Beneficial Insects

Embarking on the journey of urban gardening brings us face-to-face with nature's intricate ballet, where every creature, big or small, plays a pivotal role in the ecosystem's health and vitality. Within this verdant tapestry, beneficial insects emerge as silent guardians, their presence a testament to a garden's resilience and balance. Yet, in the bustling life of city gardens, where space is a premium and nature's balance is delicately poised, the role of these tiny allies becomes even more crucial. This narrative delves deep into the heart of urban gardening, unravelling the symbiotic relationships that sustain and enrich our green spaces, guiding us through the art and science of encouraging beneficial insects to thrive in our gardens.

Imagine your garden as a bustling city for these insects, where every bloom and leaf offers them sanctuary and sustenance. The very essence of maintaining a healthy garden ecosystem lies in understanding these creatures' roles—from the pollinators buzzing from flower to flower to the predatory insects keeping pest populations in check. But how do we turn our urban gardens into havens for these beneficial beings? The answer lies not in the application of broad-spectrum pesticides but in nurturing a space where nature's checks and balances can operate freely.

Attracting beneficial insects to the garden is akin to rolling out the red carpet for nature's helpers. It involves creating an environment that caters to their needs for food, water, and shelter. This could be as simple as planting a diverse array of flowering plants to provide nectar throughout the growing season or as strategic as designing spaces that mimic their natural habitats. But have you ever paused to wonder who these beneficial visitors are? From the hardworking bees and butterflies that ensure our plants are pollinated to the voracious ladybugs and lacewings that keep aphid populations at bay, each plays a crucial role in the garden's health.

Incorporating personal stories of urban gardeners who have successfully transformed their spaces into thriving ecosystems highlights the tangible impact of these strategies. Picture a once struggling rooftop garden now buzzing with life, its plants robust and productive, thanks to the strategic planting of marigolds and lavender to attract pollinators and deter pests. These stories not only inspire but also demonstrate the practical application of creating a garden that works in harmony with nature.

Transitioning seamlessly into the broader perspective, this narrative underscores the garden's role within the larger urban ecosystem. By fostering biodiversity through the encouragement of beneficial insects, urban gardeners contribute to the sustainability and resilience of the urban environment itself. This approach not only enhances the productivity and health of the garden but also supports the well-being of the community and the planet.

Engaging directly with readers through vivid descriptions, direct questions, and interactive scenarios, this narrative invites urban gardeners to view their gardens as ecosystems teeming with life. Varied sentence structures and an active voice keep the text dynamic and accessible, enhancing readability and drawing readers deeper into the discussion.

As we conclude, the call to action is clear: urban gardeners are empowered to make a difference, not only in their gardens but in the urban landscape at large. By embracing the principles of ecological balance and leveraging the natural pest control services of beneficial insects, we can create urban gardens that are not only productive but also vibrant examples of sustainability in action. This journey through understanding and encouraging beneficial insects in the garden is more than a gardening strategy; it's a commitment to nurturing a harmonious relationship with the natural world, right in our backyards.

Companion Planting for Pest Management

Embarking on the journey of urban gardening introduces us to a world where the growth and health of every plant are intertwined with the ecosystem around it. In this vibrant urban tableau, the ancient practice of companion planting emerges not just as a method but as a testament to the harmony possible between plants. This approach, deeply rooted in the wisdom of ages, offers a natural blueprint for managing pests and enriching the garden's biodiversity, especially in the compact spaces of the urban jungle.

Imagine your garden as a bustling community, where each plant contributes to the collective well-being, offering shelter, nutrients, or protection to its neighbour's. Here, companion planting isn't merely about placing plants side by side; it's about crafting a living mosaic where each piece supports the next. The science behind this practice is fascinating, revealing a world where plants communicate through chemical signals, deterring pests and attracting beneficial insects, all while enhancing the overall aesthetic and yield of the garden.

Consider the classic pairing of tomatoes and basil, not only for their complementary flavours but for their mutual benefit; the basil repels harmful insects while attracting pollinators, safeguarding the tomatoes. This example is just one of many, illustrating the practical application of companion planting in urban settings. Stories abound of gardeners who, even in limited spaces, have embraced this practice, transforming their balconies and rooftops into lush, productive retreats. Their experiences highlight the adaptability of companion planting strategies, whether in ground gardens, containers, or vertical plantings.

The role of companion planting in pest management cannot be overstated. Through strategic plant selection, gardeners can create an environment less hospitable to pests and more inviting to beneficial predators. This natural balance reduces the need for chemical interventions, promoting a healthier, more sustainable garden ecosystem. The diversity encouraged by companion planting not only combats pest invasions but also fortifies the garden against disease, creating a resilient, self-sustaining environment.

However, integrating companion planting into an urban garden is not without its challenges. Each plant's needs—sunlight, water, soil—must be carefully considered to ensure harmonious coexistence. Yet, the rewards of such a balanced approach are immense, offering a lesson in the beauty of biodiversity and the power of natural synergy.

As we delve into the nuances of companion planting, let's reflect on our own gardens. What combinations might work within our spaces? How can we leverage the natural relationships between plants to foster a healthier, more vibrant garden? These questions invite us to experiment, to learn from the land, and to grow not just plants but a deeper connection to the ecosystem at our doorsteps.

In cultivating a garden, we are reminded of the delicate balance of life and the importance of working with nature rather than against it. Companion planting represents a step towards a more ecological approach to gardening, one that respects and harnesses the natural relationships between plants. It's a call to urban gardeners everywhere to rethink our approach to garden design, to embrace the diversity and resilience inherent in nature, and to transform our urban spaces into thriving ecosystems.

In conclusion, the journey of integrating companion planting into urban gardens is both a challenge and an opportunity—an invitation to reimagine our relationship with nature. By fostering beneficial plant relationships, we not only enhance the health and yield of our gardens but also contribute to the sustainability of our urban environments. This narrative, rich with the experiences of fellow gardeners and grounded in the science of plant interactions, serves as a guide and inspiration. Let's embark on this journey together, nurturing our urban gardens into balanced, productive ecosystems that reflect the beauty and complexity of the natural world.

Creating a Balanced Ecosystem in Small Spaces

Diving into the essence of urban gardening reveals a world where the interplay of life forms creates a symphony of sustainability right in our backyards. Imagine transforming a small patch of the city into a vibrant ecosystem, where plants, insects, and microorganisms collaborate to foster a garden that's not just a feast for the eyes but a bastion of biodiversity. This narrative explores the journey toward creating such a balanced ecosystem in the confined spaces of urban landscapes, emphasizing the harmony achievable through mindful gardening practices.

Urban gardens, often limited by space, present a unique opportunity to demonstrate how diversity can thrive even in the smallest of areas. By selecting a variety of plants that support each other and attract beneficial insects, urban gardeners can craft living mosaics that not only beautify spaces but also serve as natural pest control agents. Imagine your garden as a bustling hub for bees, butterflies, and ladybugs, where every plant plays a role in attracting these beneficial visitors, thereby ensuring pollination and pest management naturally occur.

The role of companion planting in this ecological tapestry cannot be overstated. More than just placing plants side by side, it's about understanding the relationships between different species and how they can benefit each other. For example, the classic combination of tomatoes and basil not only enhances the flavour of your harvest but also repels pests, showcasing how strategic plant partnerships can yield multiple benefits.

In the heart of the garden, beneath the soil, lies another key player in creating a balanced ecosystem: the soil itself. Healthy soil teeming with life is the foundation upon which sustainable gardens are built.

Practices like composting and mulching enrich the soil, encouraging a diverse microbial community that supports plant health and helps ward off diseases. This underground world is a testament to the fact that the health of our gardens starts from the ground up.

Despite the challenges—such as limited light and space—innovative solutions abound. Container gardening, vertical planting, and the selection of shade-tolerant plants are just a few examples of how urban gardeners can overcome obstacles to biodiversity. Stories of resilience and creativity from the urban gardening community inspire us to view these challenges not as barriers but as invitations to innovate.

Engaging directly with the concept of the urban garden as an ecosystem, these narrative invites readers to observe, experiment, and learn. It's a call to action for gardeners to not only cultivate plants but to foster ecosystems. The rewards of such an approach extend beyond the harvest; they include the satisfaction of contributing to urban biodiversity and the joy of seeing a garden teeming with life.

As we conclude this exploration, the vision of urban gardens as ecosystems comes full circle. The journey to create a balanced ecosystem in small spaces is both a challenge and an opportunity—an opportunity to rethink our relationship with nature, to embrace the complexity of living systems, and to contribute to a sustainable future, one garden at a time. This narrative, woven from the threads of scientific insight, practical advice, and real-life success stories, serves as both a guide and an inspiration for urban gardeners to embark on their journey toward creating resilient, balanced gardens.

Conclusion

As we conclude our exploration of "Building Resilience in Your Garden," we reflect on the journey we've undertaken together. We've ventured deep into the heart of urban gardening, uncovering the principles and practices that underpin a resilient garden. This journey has revealed that resilience in gardening is about more than just surviving; it's about thriving, about creating ecosystems that support life in all its forms, from the smallest microorganisms in the soil to the people who tend to the plants.

The practices we've explored, from nurturing beneficial insects to mastering the art of companion planting, are not just techniques but a philosophy of gardening that respects and leverages the natural world's complexities. This philosophy challenges us to rethink our role as gardeners, seeing ourselves as stewards of the ecosystems under our care.

Our gardens, no matter how small, are powerful. They have the potential to contribute to the biodiversity of urban environments, to provide sanctuaries for wildlife, and to offer us a connection to the natural world that is increasingly rare in urban landscapes. As we move forward, let us carry the lessons of resilience, sustainability, and harmony with us, applying them not just in our gardens but in our lives.

This chapter is not an end but a beginning—a first step on a path that leads toward more sustainable, resilient urban gardening. As you continue on this path, remember that every plant you nurture, every insect you welcome into your garden, and every bit of soil you enrich contributes to a larger effort to bring life and resilience to our urban spaces.

Book IV: The Urban Gardener's Year

Introduction

Spring in the urban garden is a rebirth, a time when the quiet, dormant spaces of our cities come alive with the promise of growth. This chapter invites readers on a journey through the awakening of the urban garden, exploring the essential steps that transform these spaces from winter's sleep into spring's vibrant activity. From the initial soil preparation to early planting and the challenges of managing spring pests and unpredictable weather, this introduction sets the stage for a comprehensive guide to revitalizing urban gardens.

Spring: Awakening the Urban Garden

Soil Preparation and Early Planting

As the chill of winter recedes, giving way to the gentle warmth of spring, urban gardens begin to stir from their slumber. This period of renewal invites a flurry of activity, laying the groundwork for the bounty that follows. Spring in the urban garden is a time of promise, a period to embrace the new life that's about to burst forth. This narrative explores the vital steps of awakening the urban garden, from rejuvenating the soil beneath our feet to sowing the first seeds of the season and warding off the eager pests that arrive with the warmer air.

The foundation of a thriving garden is its soil, a living, breathing entity that winter has left compacted and depleted. The gardener's first task is to awaken this slumbering giant, testing its readiness to nurture new life. Enriching the garden's bed with compost and organic matter revitalizes the soil, encouraging a symphony of microbial activity essential for plant health. This process isn't just about feeding the earth; it's about reestablishing a balanced ecosystem that supports growth from the ground up.

With the soil prepared, the focus shifts to early planting. This stage requires a delicate balance, choosing plants that can withstand the cool start of spring while anticipating the warmer days ahead. Starting seeds indoors or using protective measures like cold frames can shield tender seedlings from the unpredictable moods of spring weather. This early start is crucial, providing a head start that can lead to a more fruitful harvest. However, the awakening garden also signals a feast for pests, eager to claim their share of the tender green shoots. Natural and preventative strategies become the gardener's allies, from introducing physical barriers to inviting beneficial insects that keep pest populations in check. Early vigilance and natural interventions align with the sustainable ethos of urban gardening, preserving the garden's health without resorting to chemical warfare.

Spring's capricious weather poses its own set of challenges, from sudden frosts to drenching rains. Yet, these too can be navigated with mulch to regulate soil temperature, strategic plant placement, and the creation of rain gardens to manage water surplus. Each adaptation not only mitigates the risks but also enriches the garden's resilience, turning potential setbacks into opportunities for growth. As we delve into the awakening of the urban garden, we're reminded of the cyclical nature of life and the gardener's role as both caretaker and student. The work done in the brisk days of spring sets the stage for the seasons to come, a testament to the enduring partnership between human and nature. This time of preparation and anticipation is filled with lessons on patience, resilience, and the interconnectedness of the ecosystem.

Reflecting on the journey from dormant earth to burgeoning garden, we see the promise of spring not just in the blooms and harvests that lie ahead but in the deeper understanding and connection to the natural world that gardening fosters. This awakening is more than a series of tasks; it's an annual renewal of the gardener's bond with the earth, a reaffirmation of the joy and responsibility of nurturing life in the heart of the city.

Managing Spring Pests and Weather Challenges

With the arrival of spring, the urban garden begins its transition from dormancy to vibrant life, a transformation that demands not just initial efforts in soil preparation and planting but also ongoing vigilance and care. As gardeners, our role evolves with the season, from cultivators to guardians of this burgeoning life, ensuring the garden's resilience against the unpredictable elements and challenges spring can bring.

The journey through spring in an urban garden is a delicate balance of encouragement and protection. We start by enriching the soil, our garden's foundation, with compost and organic amendments to support the young plants. But our work doesn't stop there; as the season progresses, maintaining soil health becomes a continuous task. Regular testing, the addition of natural fertilizers, and adjustments based on plant growth and health are crucial. These steps ensure that the vibrant start we've given our garden can sustain the plants as they mature.

Water management, too, takes centre stage as spring's unpredictable weather patterns can bring too much rain or sudden dry spells. Efficient use of water, from rainwater harvesting to mulching for moisture retention, not only conserves this precious resource but also supports stable growth. Similarly, understanding and leveraging microclimates within the garden can shield our young charges from late frosts or the chill of spring nights, employing strategies like cloches or row covers to provide a warm embrace.

The awakening garden also signals a feast for pests, those uninvited guests who are drawn to the tender new growth. Here, the narrative deepens into the complexity of pest management, where fostering an environment that welcomes beneficial insects becomes a sustainable strategy for natural balance. Biological control, such as introducing or attracting predators of common pests, and integrated pest management practices emphasize a mindful approach to garden care, minimizing harm while maintaining the health of our garden ecosystem.

As our plants grow, so too does the sense of community around the garden. Sharing knowledge, experiences, and the fruits of our labour with neighbour's or through community garden initiatives enriches not just our gardens but our lives. This communal aspect of urban gardening fosters a broader understanding of our role not just as individual gardeners but as part of a larger ecosystem, where our choices impact not only our garden but the urban environment as a whole.

Looking ahead, the efforts we make in spring set the stage for the coming seasons. Planning for summer crops, starting warm-season seeds, and preparing for the garden's next phases are all part of the spring gardening journey. These actions are not just about anticipation but are a reflection of the cycle of gardening itself—a cycle of preparation, growth, and renewal.

As we reflect on the journey through spring in the urban garden, it's clear that this season is a chapter of both challenge and reward. The transformation of the garden from a quiet winter plot to a thriving spring ecosystem is a testament to the gardener's dedication and the resilience of nature. Spring in the urban garden is a time of growth, not just for the plants but for the gardeners themselves, who through their efforts, deepen their connection to the natural world. This season of awakening is just the beginning of a rich narrative of urban gardening, one that continues to unfold with each passing day.

Conclusion

As the chapter on "Spring: Awakening the Urban Garden" draws to a close, we reflect on the journey from the quiet anticipation of early spring to the bustling life that now fills urban gardens. This conclusion reiterates the importance of the groundwork laid during this season—the careful preparation of soil, the strategic early planting, and the vigilant management of pests and weather—that ensures the garden's vitality. It celebrates the transformation achieved through dedication and attunement to nature's rhythms, offering readers not just a set of gardening tasks but an invitation to participate in the cycle of life that unfolds in their urban oases.

Looking forward, the conclusion inspires readers to continue nurturing their gardens with an eye toward the future, emphasizing that the efforts of spring are just the beginning of a rewarding gardening year.

Introduction

As the urban landscape basks in the full glory of summer, gardens become centres of life and activity, heralding a season of peak production. This introduction sets the stage for a deep dive into the heart of summer gardening, emphasizing the transformative power of this season on urban green spaces. It beckons readers to journey through the myriad challenges and opportunities that summer brings, from the scorching heat to the threat of pests, all while navigating the quest for a continuous harvest.

The narrative begins by painting a vivid picture of the urban garden in summer—a lush, vibrant oasis amid the concrete, where the air is thick with the scent of blooming flowers and the promise of fresh produce. It frames the season as a critical time for gardeners, a period requiring keen insight, adaptability, and a proactive approach to ensure the garden's health and productivity.

Summer: Peak Production

Optimizing Water Use During Hot Months

As the days lengthen and the warmth of the sun envelops the city, urban gardens enter their most dynamic phase of the year: the summer season. This period stands not only as a test of resilience for both the gardener and the garden but also as a time of abundant rewards. The shift into summer requires a strategic approach to gardening, one that addresses the challenges of heat, water management, and pests, all while ensuring a continuous harvest of fresh, vibrant produce.

In the heart of summer, water becomes the lifeblood of the urban garden. The rising temperatures and increased sunlight exposure dramatically escalate the garden's thirst. Addressing this critical need without succumbing to wastefulness is paramount. Techniques such as establishing a drip irrigation system, which directs water efficiently and directly to plant roots, become invaluable. Moreover, the practice of collecting rainwater, a method as ancient as gardening itself, finds new relevance in the urban context as a sustainable resource for hydration. The application of mulch around plants serves a dual purpose in this season: it conserves moisture by reducing evaporation and also provides a barrier against the heat, keeping the soil cool and hospitable for root growth.

With the garden fully awakened, summer planting strategies come to the forefront. Succession planting, the method of planting crops at staggered intervals, ensures that as one harvest concludes, another begins, maintaining a cycle of production that can fill the summer months with a variety of fresh produce. Choosing the right crops for the season—those that thrive in the warmth and light of summer—becomes a dance of timing and selection. From leafy greens that mature quickly to heat-loving nightshades like tomatoes and peppers, the urban garden becomes a testament to diversity and abundance.

However, the bounty of summer does not come without its adversaries. Heat stress and pests emerge as significant challenges, threatening to undermine the garden's productivity. Techniques to combat these threats are varied and holistic. Providing shade during the hottest parts of the day can protect plants from the stress of excessive heat, while natural pest management strategies—such as encouraging beneficial insects that prey on common pests— enhance the garden's ecological balance without resorting to harmful chemicals.

This journey through the summer season in the urban garden is as much about adaptation and learning as it is about gardening itself. It's a time when the gardener's skills are honed, and the connection between the gardener and the garden deepens. The challenges faced and overcome enrich the experience, making the successes all the more rewarding.

As summer matures and the cycle of growth continues, the urban garden stands as a vibrant oasis in the heat of the city, a testament to the gardener's dedication and the resilience of nature. The lessons of the summer garden—water management, strategic planting, and ecological pest control—reflect a broader philosophy of gardening that respects the rhythms of the natural world and seeks harmony within the urban environment. This season of peak production is not just about the abundance it brings but also about the enduring principles it teaches, principles that guide the urban gardener toward a sustainable, productive partnership with the earth.

Summer Planting for Continuous Harvest

As summer unfurls its full might over the urban landscape, gardens become arenas of both lush growth and intense challenge. This pivotal season, with its longer days and warmer nights, calls for a gardener's careful attention and adaptability. The narrative of summer gardening is a tale of a balancing act—nurturing the garden to its peak production while guarding against the season's harsher aspects.

In the heart of summer, the wise management of water stands as the cornerstone of garden health and vitality. Innovative practices such as drip irrigation exemplify the precision needed to sustain plants without wastage, ensuring water reaches directly to the roots where it's most needed. Meanwhile, the ancient practice of rainwater harvesting reemerges as a beacon of sustainability, capturing the season's sporadic downpours for later use. These methods not only conserve a crucial resource but also underscore the garden as a paradigm of ecological resilience.

The rhythm of planting during these warm months is attuned to the season's cadence. Succession planting becomes a strategic endeavor, ensuring that as one crop reaches its end, another begins, offering a continuous bounty. The garden, in this light, is a dynamic entity, ever-changing and always growing. The selection of heat-tolerant plants and the timing of their planting are critical, ensuring the garden remains productive and vibrant throughout the season.

Yet, summer's warmth does not come without its trials. Heat stress and pests emerge as significant challenges, threatening the well-being of the garden. The narrative here shifts to the strategies of mitigation and balance, employing shade cloths to protect plants from the sun's intensity and embracing natural pest control methods to maintain ecological equilibrium. These approaches highlight a garden in harmony, where challenges are met with thoughtful, sustainable solutions.

As the story of summer gardening unfolds, it becomes clear that the urban garden is more than a space of cultivation—it's a microcosm of life, reflecting broader environmental truths and challenges. The urban gardener, in turn, is seen not merely as a caretaker of plants but as a steward of the land, contributing to a sustainable future through mindful gardening practices.

Reflecting on the summer journey, it's evident that this season, for all its intensity, is a profoundly rewarding time. It reaffirms the garden's place as an oasis of abundance, resilience, and beauty amid the urban sprawl. The lessons of summer—water conservation, strategic planting, and ecological pest management—are invaluable, laying a foundation for not only the current season's success but also the health and productivity of the garden in the years to come.

In embracing the challenges and joys of summer gardening, we engage in a deeper dialogue with nature, learning, growing, and ultimately flourishing alongside our garden. This narrative of peak production is a testament to the enduring power of dedicated stewardship, a reminder of the beauty and abundance that awaits those who garden with intention and car

Dealing with Heat Stress and Summer Pests

In the heart of summer, urban gardens enter a critical phase of growth and challenge, where the balmy days and warm nights set the stage for both abundant harvests and potential adversities. This season, vibrant with life, demands a gardener's strategic insight and adaptability to ensure the garden not only survives but thrives under the summer sun.

Efficient water use emerges as a paramount concern during these months, as the rising temperatures escalate the garden's thirst. Innovative irrigation techniques, such as drip systems, become indispensable, delivering water directly to the roots where it's most needed and minimizing waste. The practice of rainwater harvesting aligns with sustainable gardening ethics, turning sporadic downpours into a valuable resource. Moreover, the strategic application of mulch around plants plays a dual role, conserving moisture while shielding the soil from the sun's intensity, ensuring the garden remains a sanctuary of growth.

As the season progresses, the concept of a continuous harvest takes centre stage. Through thoughtful planning and succession planting, the garden can yield a steady supply of fresh produce. The selection of crops adapted to the warmth of summer, coupled with staggered planting schedules, ensures that as one crop matures, another begins to flourish. This dynamic approach not only maximizes the garden's productivity but also enhances its resilience, making it a testament to the careful orchestration of nature and nurture.

However, the warmth that stimulates growth also invites challenges, particularly heat stress and pests, which can threaten the garden's vitality. Here, the narrative shifts to protective strategies that safeguard the garden's bounty. Employing shade cloths during the peak sun hours and optimizing watering routines to avoid evaporation are critical measures to combat heat stress. Simultaneously, an integrated pest management approach, emphasizing organic and natural remedies, ensures that the garden remains a balanced ecosystem, where beneficial predators and plant health coexist harmoniously.

Navigating the summer in the urban garden is not just about overcoming obstacles but also about embracing the season's opportunities for growth and learning. It's a time when the garden becomes a living classroom, revealing lessons in sustainability, resilience, and the intricate dance between human effort and natural processes.

Conclusion

The conclusion of the chapter on "Summer: Peak Production" is a reflective and forward-looking piece that encapsulates the journey through the summer gardening season. It highlights the achievements and learning moments, acknowledging the gardener's efforts to maintain balance in the face of summer's intensity. This section reinforces the value of the lessons learned during these months, emphasizing their applicability to future gardening endeavors and their contribution to a more sustainable, resilient urban ecosystem.

Celebrating the bounty of summer, the conclusion also invites readers to savor the rewards of their labor—be it the harvest, the enhanced beauty of their space, or the deepened connection with nature. It underscores the cyclical nature of gardening, where each season builds upon the last, and each challenge overcome enriches the gardener's experience and knowledge.

Introduction

As the warmth of summer wanes and the first cool whispers of autumn begin to weave through the urban garden, a profound shift occurs. This is the season when the vibrant energy of growth makes way for a quieter, more reflective time—a period of preparation and transition. Autumn in the garden is not just a change in the season; it's a pivotal chapter in the life cycle of the garden and the gardener alike.

This season brings the garden's bounty to the forefront, with harvests that are the culmination of months of care, patience, and growth. But as each fruit is picked and vegetable gathered, there's an underlying rhythm of preparation beating at the heart of these tasks. The garden, so alive with the colours and textures of autumn, now asks for attention of a different kind. It's time to preserve the abundance, to plant the seeds of future growth, and to prepare the soil and plants for the coming rest of winter.

Harvesting in autumn is a labor filled with gratitude and reflection. Each crop collected is a reminder of the summer past and the cycle of life that sustains us. Preserving this bounty—through canning, drying, and fermenting—is not just a practical act of preparation; it's a ritual that connects us to generations past and traditions that have stood the test of time.

Planting for autumn and winter is an act of hope, a gesture that speaks to the gardener's belief in the future. It's a commitment to the garden's continued vitality, ensuring that even as the cold sets in, the promise of growth remains alive under the frost.

And in preparing the soil and garden for winter, gardeners engage in a thoughtful process of care and stewardship. This work, often seen as the closing of the garden's year, is in fact a foundational step towards the next cycle of growth. It's a time to enrich the soil, protect the plants, and lay the groundwork for the spring to come.

Autumn: Preparing for Rest

Harvesting and Preserving Your Bounty

As the vibrant energy of summer gives way to the mellow tones of autumn, the urban garden enters a period of transition. This time of year is not just about the harvest and the preparation for the colder months ahead; it's a celebration of the cycle of growth and rest. Autumn in the garden is a beautiful juxtaposition of abundance and preparation for dormancy, a time to gather the fruits of summer's labor while gently guiding the garden toward its winter rest.

The first chill of autumn air brings with it the task of harvesting. This section delves into the techniques and timing for gathering crops at their peak, ensuring the hard work of the preceding months is captured in the flavors and textures of the harvest. But the abundance of autumn requires foresight—preserving the excess becomes an art form in itself. Techniques such as canning, drying, and freezing are explored, offering readers a guide to enjoying the summer's bounty long after the garden has been put to bed.

Yet, even as we harvest, the cycle of growth continues. Planting in autumn for the next season's harvest challenges the conventional notion of gardening as a predominantly spring and summer activity. This narrative thread introduces the concept of overwintering crops—garlic, onions, and certain hardy greens—that benefit from winter under the soil, ready to burst forth as the first signs of spring appear. It also touches on the importance of cover crops to protect and enrich the soil, ensuring it remains vibrant and alive even as the garden above starts to quieten.

The soul of the garden lies in its soil, and autumn is a crucial time for ensuring its health and vitality. This part of the narrative focuses on the steps needed to protect and enrich the garden's foundation. Mulching, adding compost, and other soil amendments are discussed, with an emphasis on sustainable practices that nourish the soil. This preparation not only safeguards the garden through the winter months but also sets the stage for the next cycle of growth, embodying the gardener's commitment to the earth and its stewardship.

autumn in the urban garden is a reflective time, a period to take stock of the year's successes and learnings while looking forward to the cycles yet to come. It's a season filled with the satisfaction of harvest, the promise of future growth, and the beauty of nature's rhythms. The gardener, in turn, becomes a caretaker of these cycles, guiding the garden through its phases of activity and rest with a mindful eye on sustainability and the deep connection between humans and the natural world.

as the narrative on autumn gardening comes to a close, it celebrates the season not just as an end but as a pivotal moment of preparation and transition. Autumn's tasks—harvesting, preserving, planting, and preparing—are acts of love and foresight, ensuring the garden remains a source of sustenance and joy. This chapter on "Autumn: Preparing for Rest" underscores the cyclical nature of gardening, where every end is a beginning, and every act of preparation is a step towards future abundance.

Planting for Autumn and Winter

As autumn unfurls its palette across the urban landscape, gardens enter a pivotal phase. This season isn't merely a closure but a preparation, a crucial period that ensures the continuity of life beneath the soil even as the world above starts to slumber. The essence of autumn gardening lies in three core activities: harvesting what has matured, sowing seeds for the future, and fortifying the garden against the impending cold.

The culmination of summer's toil, the harvest, begins with the careful collection of fruits, vegetables, and herbs. Gardeners, with their hands seasoned by the soil, engage in the delicate task of picking, choosing the perfect moment when ripeness meets readiness. This period is as much about the physical gathering of produce as it is about preserving the abundance. Techniques passed down through generations— canning, drying, fermenting—come to the forefront, transforming the harvest into forms that can weather the scarcity of winter.

Even as the present bounty demands attention, thoughts turn to future harvests. The cooler days of autumn provide a window for planting crops that thrive in the chill or lie dormant until spring's thaw. This forward-looking act, planting bulbs and late-season greens, is a testament to the gardener's optimism and trust in the cycles of growth. It's a commitment to the garden's future, ensuring that as one cycle concludes, another is set to begin.

Preparation for winter's rest encompasses more than just the soil; it's a holistic approach to safeguarding the garden's vitality. Enriching the earth with compost, covering beds with mulch, and protecting sensitive plants are acts of stewardship. They are measures that not only insulate the garden from frost but also enrich the soil, building a foundation for the next season's growth.

This transition period is reflective, marked by the slowing pace of growth and the preparation for winter. It's a time when the gardener's efforts pivot from cultivation to preservation, ensuring that the garden, though resting, remains a place of potential. Autumn, with its focus on harvesting, planting, and preparing, bridges the bounty of the past with the promise of the future, embodying the perpetual cycle of life in the garden.

Soil and Garden Preparation for Winter

In the heart of autumn, the urban garden is a testament to the cycle of growth, maturity, and renewal. This season, defined by the crispness in the air and the golden hue of leaves, marks a period of significant transition for gardeners and their cherished spaces. It's a time when the fruits of summer's labor are gathered, the plans for the cold months are set in motion, and the garden beds are lovingly prepared for the winter's rest.

As the days shorten and the garden's pace slows, there's a profound sense of both culmination and preparation. Harvesting becomes not just an act of gathering but a celebration of the season's bounty. This is the time when tomatoes, squash, beans, and countless other crops are picked, each vegetable and fruit telling a story of the months gone by. But beyond the immediate joy of the harvest lies the task of preservation—canning, drying, and fermenting—ensuring that the flavors of autumn can be savored well into the winter months.

Yet, autumn is not merely an ending but a bridge to future growth. The act of planting during this season—be it the hardy greens that will brave the coming frosts or the bulbs that will lie dormant until spring—speaks to the gardener's forward-looking vision. It's an acknowledgment that even as one cycle ends, another awaits its turn, ready to unfurl with the warmth of the coming spring.

Equally critical is the preparation of the soil and garden for the colder months. This involves more than simply clearing away the remnants of summer's abundance; it's a time for enriching the garden with compost, for protecting the soil with mulch, and for ensuring that the hard-won gains of the past seasons are safeguarded against the winter's chill. Such tasks are performed not with a sense of finality but with the knowledge that they are essential steps in the garden's ongoing journey.

Through these endeavours—harvesting and preserving the bounty, planting for the future, and preparing the garden for winter—the urban gardener engages deeply with the rhythms of the natural world. Autumn becomes a canvas upon which the cycle of life, with its ebbs and flows, is vividly illustrated. It's a season that calls for reflection on the successes and lessons of the year, even as it demands a forward-thinking approach to the seasons yet to come.

Conclusion

As the chapter of autumn closes, the garden settles into a period of rest, but the work done during these months of preparation carries a lasting impact. The tasks of harvesting, preserving, planting, and preparing are acts woven with the threads of reflection, hope, and continuity. They are the gardener's response to the rhythm of the seasons, a rhythm that pulses with the promise of renewal and growth.

Autumn in the garden is a testament to the cycles of nature—a reminder that every ending is poised on the cusp of a new beginning. The work of this season, rich with the fruits of the past and the seeds of the future, is a profound expression of the gardener's role as both caretaker and participant in the dance of life.

This season of preparation is an invitation to look forward, to plan for the garden's reawakening even as it enters a period of dormancy. It's a time to celebrate the bounty of the harvest, to honor the traditions of preservation, and to engage in the thoughtful stewardship of the living earth.

As the garden rests, the gardener reflects on the year gone by and looks ahead to the future. The quiet of winter offers a space for planning, for dreaming of the next season's garden, and for finding joy in the anticipation of what's to come. Autumn, with its focus on preparation and rest, is not just a conclusion but a crucial step towards the garden's renewal.

Introduction

Winter descends on the garden not with the finality of an end but with the quiet promise of future abundance. As the vibrant hues of autumn fade to the subdued palette of winter, the urban garden enters a time of apparent rest. Yet, beneath this serene stillness, a profound transformation is underway. For the gardener, this season is a sacred pause, offering a moment to step back, to reflect on the year's successes, and learn from its trials. It's a period marked by the gathering of insights from past seasons—each plant, pest, and plot contributing to a growing repository of knowledge.

But winter is more than a time for reflection; it's a season of active preparation and planning. With the garden lying dormant, the gardener is free to dream, to imagine what might be. It's a time for pouring over seed catalogues, for sketching out new designs, for considering the balance of the ecosystem within the garden's borders. The quiet of winter provides the perfect backdrop for this creative envisioning, free from the immediate demands of tending and toil.

Winter: Planning and Preparation

Reflecting on Past Seasons: Lessons Learned

in the heart of winter, when the garden lies dormant beneath a pristine blanket of snow, the urban gardener finds themselves at a pivotal juncture of the year. This season, often perceived as a pause, is rich with potential and purpose. It's a time for introspection, for learning from the past, and for meticulous planning for the seasons ahead. Winter, with its inherent quiet and slowed pace, offers a unique opportunity to deepen our connection with gardening, not through daily toil in the soil, but through the thoughtful preparation and planning that are just as crucial to a garden's success.

Winter invites gardeners to settle into the comfort of their warm homes, surrounded by seed catalogues, garden journals, and the vibrant memories of the garden's previous iterations. This is the time to reflect on the past growing seasons, to sift through what worked and what didn't. Perhaps a certain crop thrived unexpectedly, offering a bountiful harvest that brought joy and sustenance. Or maybe a battle with pests provided valuable lessons on natural pest control methods. Each season, with its triumphs and challenges, contributes to the gardener's evolving understanding of their space and craft.

With reflections in mind, the focus shifts to planning for the future. This involves more than just choosing which seeds to sow. It's about envisioning the garden in its entirety, considering rotations for soil health, integrating companion plants for natural pest management, and perhaps planning new sections for biodiversity. Winter's respite allows gardeners to research, to dream, and to sketch out plans that will transform into vibrant life come spring. This period of planning is as creative as it is strategic, fueled by the lessons of past seasons and the endless possibilities of those to come.

The quiet of winter also opens up space for projects that lay the groundwork for a productive garden. Whether it's building new raised beds, setting up a system for rainwater harvesting, or starting a compost bin, these projects are investments in the garden's infrastructure and sustainability. They are acts of hope and preparation, done with the anticipation of spring's arrival. Each project, no matter how small, is a step toward a more resilient and thriving garden.

As the chapter on winter concludes, it's clear that this season's quiet is deceptive. Beneath its still surface, a flurry of activity and preparation sets the stage for the garden's future success. Winter is a time to embrace the slow rhythms of nature, to learn, plan, and prepare with intention. It's a season that underscores the truth that every gardener knows: even in rest, there's growth happening, unseen, laying the foundation for the abundance and beauty of the year ahead.

Planning for the Next Growing Season

As the vibrant energy of the garden wanes into the serene stillness of winter, the urban gardener steps into a season of profound reflection and meticulous preparation. This period, often cloaked in the quiet white of snow, is far from a mere hiatus in the cycle of growth. It's a pivotal chapter in the gardener's year, offering a precious moment to pause, take stock, and plan with intention for the burgeoning life of spring just beneath the surface.

Winter draws the gardener inward, encouraging a thoughtful review of the year's garden. It's a time to celebrate the triumphs—perhaps a bountiful harvest of tomatoes that seemed almost miraculous in its abundance—and to learn from the trials, such as the challenge of contending with an unforeseen pest. This season of reflection is not just about reminiscing; it's a vital process of gathering insights, understanding the rhythm and needs of the garden, and acknowledging the lessons that each plant, pest, and plot of soil has to offer.

Armed with knowledge and inspired by the dormant potential around them, the gardener begins the creative endeavor of planning for the next growing season. This involves more than selecting seeds; it's about envisioning the future of the garden in its entirety. Winter provides the calm necessary to consider new layouts, to research sustainable gardening practices, and to dream up innovative projects that will enhance the garden's ecosystem. Every catalogue perused and plan drawn is a step closer to realizing the garden's future splendour.

The cold months also present an opportunity for the gardener to undertake projects that lay the groundwork for success come spring. From constructing a trellis that will support climbing vines to repairing garden tools, each task is an investment in the garden's future productivity. Perhaps there's a story of building a compost bin, a simple structure that not only recycles garden and kitchen waste but also symbolizes the cycle of life and renewal at the heart of gardening.

As the narrative unfolds, it becomes clear that winter, with its planning and preparation, is as much a season of growth as any other. It's a time when the gardener grows in knowledge, foresight, and connection to the earth. The quiet of winter allows for a deeper understanding of the natural world and one's place within it, fostering a sense of stewardship and a commitment to cultivating not just a garden, but a thriving, sustainable ecosystem.

The chapter closes on a note of anticipation. The work done during the winter months—reflecting, planning, and preparing—sets the stage for the renewal of spring. The garden, though presently quiet, is poised for a burst of life, with each seed, plan, and project a promise of the beauty and abundance to come. Winter, in its stillness, is a testament to the gardener's enduring hope and the perpetual cycle of life that turns within the garden.

Winter Projects for the Urban Gardener

Winter in the urban garden is a silent revolution, a time when the earth may seem at rest, but the gardener is abuzz with activity, reflection, and preparation. This season, though devoid of the garden's lush visuals, is rich with potential and purpose. It's during these colder months that the gardener lays the groundwork for future growth, drawing lessons from the past and setting intentions for the year ahead.

begin by diving into the introspective aspect of winter. Reflect on the garden's past season, acknowledging both its triumphs and challenges. Perhaps recount a personal narrative of a particular crop that taught a valuable lesson in resilience or adaptability. These reflections are not mere reminiscences but stepping stones for future growth, providing invaluable insights that will inform the garden's evolution.

With lessons learned firmly in hand, shift focus to the forward-looking process of planning the next growing season. This is a time for dreaming and scheming, for imagining what the garden could become. Describe the process of selecting new plant varieties, considering companion planting strategies, and perhaps even redesigning the garden layout. Highlight the importance of sustainability and biodiversity in these plans, making the case for a garden that not only thrives but also supports the local ecosystem.

Winter's projects are the gardener's investment in the garden's future success. From building raised beds to optimizing a composting system, each task is undertaken with a vision of the spring to come. Illustrate the process and purpose behind one or two key winter projects, showcasing how these efforts contribute to a more productive and resilient garden. These narratives should underscore the connection between the gardener's winter labors and the anticipation of spring's rewards.

Amid the physical tasks of winter, there's also an internal journey happening for the gardener. Discuss the cultivation of patience and perspective during these quieter months. Winter teaches the gardener to slow down, to plan with care, and to embrace the slower pace of nature's cycle. This period of forced pause is as crucial to the gardener's growth as it is to the garden's future flourishing.

Conclude with the palpable sense of anticipation that builds as winter gradually yields to the first signs of spring. The planning, reflection, and groundwork of the winter months prepare both the gardener and the garden for the burst of life to come. This final section should evoke the excitement and potential that lies in waiting, ready to spring forth from the well-prepared soil.

Conclusion

As winter's chill begins to wane and the first signs of spring whisper promises of renewal, the gardener finds themselves at the threshold of a new cycle of growth, armed with the plans and preparations laid down during the colder months. The lessons gleaned from reflecting on past seasons form the foundation of these future endeavours. With a deeper understanding of the garden's rhythms and needs, the gardener is better equipped to nurture and sustain the vibrant life that will soon emerge.

The projects undertaken over the winter, from the construction of new beds to the optimization of composting practices, are about to prove their worth. These are not just tasks completed but investments made into the health and productivity of the garden. They are acts of faith in the future, reflecting a commitment to stewardship and a belief in the garden's potential.

Winter, with its introspective quiet and its focus on planning and preparation, is an essential chapter in the gardener's year. It is a time that teaches patience, fosters creativity, and builds anticipation for the abundance to come. As we move forward into the bustle of the growing season, we carry with us the plans laid and the lessons learned in the stillness of winter, ready to bring our garden dreams to fruition.

Book V: Beyond the Garden

Introduction

As the garden basks in the fullness of summer, every leaf and vine heavy with the promise of harvest, we stand on the cusp of a season of abundance. The chapter you are about to explore delves into the timeless rituals of harvest and preservation, practices that weave through the history of humankind, connecting us to the very essence of survival and sustenance. Here, we embark on a journey that transcends the mere act of collecting the fruits of our labour. It's a foray into an art form cultivated through generations, an art that marries the science of timing with the culinary alchemy of preservation.

Harvesting, as you will see, is not merely about picking; it is about capturing the moment. It's a delicate balance of timing, technique, and intuition, ensuring each fruit, vegetable, and herb is gathered at its nutritional and flavourful zenith. This chapter aims to guide you through this dance with nature, offering insights into recognizing the subtle cues of readiness in your garden's bounty.

Yet, what follows the harvest is equally a testament to our ingenuity and desire to hold onto the ephemeral beauty of the growing season. Preservation—be it through freezing, fermenting, canning, or drying—is the bridge between the abundance of today and the scarcity of tomorrow. It is our rebellion against the temporal, a means to extend the life and vitality of our harvests, allowing us to taste the sweetness of summer even in the depths of winter.

In this narrative, we not only provide practical advice and techniques but also seek to instil a deeper appreciation for the rhythms of nature and our place within them. This chapter is an invitation to view the acts of harvesting and preservation as more than just tasks—it's a call to participate in a cycle of renewal and gratitude, to nourish not just the body but the soul.

I.   Harvest and Preservation

Harvesting Techniques for Peak Flavour and Nutrition

The essence of a successful garden is not merely in its growth but in the timely and careful harvest of its yield. As the seasons turn, the garden transforms into a palette of ripeness, each fruit, vegetable, and herb whispering the perfect moment for harvest. This chapter delves into the nuanced art of harvesting, guiding you through techniques that ensure each pick reaches its fullest potential in flavour and nutritional value.

Harvesting is a dance with time, requiring a keen sense of when each crop is at its peak. For vegetables like zucchini and cucumbers, the best flavours are captured when they are young and tender. In contrast, root vegetables like carrots and beets store their full sweetness when allowed to mature under the soil's cool embrace. Fruits, from tomatoes to apples, share their best taste and nutritional benefits when harvested at the peak of ripeness, a moment often marked by a deepening of color and a gentle yield to the touch.

Beyond timing, the method of harvest plays a pivotal role in preserving the integrity and future productivity of your plants. Gentle hands can ensure leafy greens continue to produce and berries remain unbruised. Techniques vary from the simple twist-off method for ripe tomatoes to the careful use of shears for herbs and greens, minimizing stress on the plants and ensuring a continued yield.

With baskets full, the focus shifts to preservation, capturing the essence of your harvest for the seasons beyond. Freezing stands out for its simplicity and effectiveness, locking in flavor and nutritional value with minimal fuss. Techniques range from flash-freezing berries on trays to blanching vegetables before they hit the cold. Each method is tailored to the unique needs of your produce, ensuring that the vibrant flavors of summer can grace your winter table.

The ancient art of fermentation not only preserves your harvest but also enhances its nutritional profile. Simple to start yet complex in its outcomes, fermentation can transform cabbage into sauerkraut and cucumbers into pickles, introducing a world of flavours and probiotics into your diet. This section guides you through the basics, from creating the right salt brine to understanding the signs of successful fermentation.

Harvesting and preservation are the culmination of a gardener's year, a testament to the care and attention poured into the soil. These practices are not just about sustenance but about continuing a cycle of growth, nutrition, and enjoyment that ties us to the rhythms of the natural world. As you master these techniques, you become a steward of these cycles, ensuring that the bounty of your garden nourishes not just your body but also your connection to the earth.

Preserving Your Harvest: From Freezing to Fermenting

As the gardening season wanes and the final harvests are brought in, the task of preserving the abundance becomes the gardener's focus. It's a time-honoured ritual, linking us to generations past and ensuring that the fruits of our labor nourish us through the colder months. This chapter delves into the complementary methods of freezing and fermenting, each a guardian of flavor and nutrition, capturing the essence of summer's bounty. Freezing is perhaps the most direct bridge between the freshness of harvest and the desire for preservation. It's a method that suspends time, locking in both the peak flavor and nutritional content of fruits and vegetables. The process begins with selection, choosing produce at its prime, and often involves a simple but crucial step: blanching.

Blanching, the brief plunge into boiling water followed by a rapid cool-down, not only preserves colour and texture but also halts enzymatic actions that can diminish flavour and nutrients. Fruits, meanwhile, might be treated with ascorbic acid solutions to preserve colour and taste before being laid out on trays to freeze individually. This ensures that berries, peach slices, or plum halves can be easily used in portions, free from clumps, ready to be summoned forth from their frozen state to brighten a midwinter meal.

Fermentation is an alchemy of the culinary world, a transformation guided by microorganisms that not only extends shelf life but enhances nutritional value. This process, grounded in the natural tendency of foods to ferment, is harnessed and controlled by the gardener-preserver to yield results as varied as the crisp tang of sauerkraut from cabbage or the spicy depth of kimchi. Fermentation isn't just preservation; it's a cultivation of flavor and health, introducing beneficial probiotics into our diets. The key to successful fermentation lies in the balance of salt and temperature, creating an environment where beneficial bacteria thrive. As vegetables are submerged in brine or their juices, they begin a slow transformation, breaking down sugars into acids, preserving the vegetables, and creating complex, layered flavors.

The acts of freezing and fermenting do more than just preserve food; they connect us to the cycles of the seasons and the traditions of our ancestors. These methods, while seemingly simple, are rich with the wisdom of past generations and the innovation of the present. They remind us that at the heart of preservation lies not just the desire to nourish our bodies but to celebrate the bounty of the earth, to honor the cycles of growth and rest, and to share this abundance with those we love.

As we master these methods, our pantries become more than just storage; they transform into a symphony of flavors waiting to be rediscovered. Each jar of fermented vegetables, each packet of frozen berries is a note in a larger composition of our culinary lives, ready to be brought forth and savored. The practice of preservation is both a grounding in the present moment and a reaching back through time, a celebration of abundance and a preparation for the future. In embracing the twin practices of freezing and fermenting, we ensure that the work of our hands and the bounty of the garden continues to sustain and delight us, no matter the season. This chapter, dedicated to the art of preservation, is more than a guide—it's an invitation to participate in the timeless dance of harvest and nourishment, a dance that sustains not just our bodies but our connection to the earth and to each other.

Conclusion

As the final pages of this chapter turn, we find ourselves not at the end of a journey but at a vantage point, looking back on the path traversed and ahead to the cycles yet to come. Harvest and preservation are not just seasonal activities but foundational elements of a sustainable life, intertwined with the natural world and our human traditions. Through the guidance offered on harvesting techniques for peak flavour and nutrition, and the exploration of preservation methods from freezing to fermenting, we've embarked on a journey that spans seasons and generations.

This chapter aims to equip you with the knowledge to capture the essence of your garden, extending the joy and sustenance it brings into every season. But beyond the practical, it has sought to weave a narrative of connection—a reminder that with each fruit picked and jar sealed, we partake in rituals as old as agriculture itself, grounding us to the earth and to each other.

In the quiet moments spent in the garden or kitchen, we find ourselves part of a larger story, one of resilience, creativity, and care. The acts of harvesting and preserving are declarations of our commitment to nourishing our families, stewarding the environment, and honouring the legacy of those who taught us these skills.

As we close this chapter, let us carry forward not just the techniques and recipes contained within these pages but a renewed sense of purpose and connection. May the rhythms of harvest and preservation become markers of our year, punctuating our days with the tangible rewards of our labour and the intangible blessings of belonging to a community of growers and makers?

In the cycle of seasons, each ending is but a prelude to another beginning. So too, the conclusion of this exploration marks the start of your next season of growth. Armed with the insights and inspirations from this chapter, may you approach each harvest with a keen eye and each act of preservation with a joyful heart, confident in the knowledge that you are part of a timeless continuum of harvest and renewal.

Introduction

In the midst of the urban sprawl, where concrete often overshadows green, community gardens emerge as vibrant testaments to the power of collective action and green-thumbed dedication. These spaces are not merely oases in the desert of the city; they are the bedrock of community building, environmental education, and a shared commitment to sustainable urban living. This chapter delves into the heart of urban gardening, exploring how these communal spaces cultivate more than just plants—they foster connections, resilience, and a profound sense of belonging among city dwellers. From the initial stirrings of interest in a vacant lot to the flourishing of a fully realized garden that feeds bodies and souls alike, we embark on a journey through the transformative impact of community gardens on individuals and urban landscapes alike.

Community and Urban Gardening

Building Community Through Urban Gardening

In the heart of the city, amidst the hustle and bustle of daily life, urban gardens emerge as oases of tranquillity and greenery. These pockets of nature do more than just beautify the urban landscape; they serve as vital platforms for community building and engagement. This chapter explores the transformative power of urban gardening, illuminating how these green spaces foster connections, promote wellness, and become catalysts for social change. Urban gardening starts with a seed, both literal and metaphorical—a seed that, when planted in the fertile ground of community engagement, grows into something much larger than the sum of its parts. This section delves into the origins of urban gardening movements, tracing their roots back to community efforts aimed at addressing urban decay, food deserts, and the need for green spaces. It celebrates the visionaries who saw the potential for gardens to bring people together, creating verdant gathering spots in the grey of the city.

As urban gardening initiatives take root, they attract a diverse cross-section of city dwellers, from seasoned horticulturists to novices eager to dig their hands into the soil. This diversity enriches the garden with a variety of perspectives, experiences, and skills, making the garden a hub of shared knowledge and mutual learning. Highlight stories of community gardens that have transformed neglected plots into vibrant centres of life, where neighbors meet, friendships bloom, and a sense of community flourishes. Participation in community gardens and initiatives is as varied as the plants that grow within them. Some find solace in the solitude of tending to their plots, while others thrive in collaborative projects, from building raised beds to organizing farmer's markets. Discuss how individuals can get involved, emphasizing the inclusive nature of these spaces. Address the challenges and rewards of participation, showcasing how collective efforts lead to sustainable, community-driven success.

Urban gardening's impact extends beyond the confines of the garden itself, influencing broader community and city-wide initiatives. Gardens become living classrooms for environmental education, platforms for advocating sustainability, and models for green urban planning. They also play a critical role in addressing urban food insecurity and providing fresh produce to those in need. Examine partnerships between gardens and local institutions, illustrating how these collaborations amplify the positive effects of urban gardening.

In conclusion, reflect on the harvest yielded by urban gardening efforts—not just the fruits, vegetables, and flowers, but the strengthened community bonds, the greened cityscapes, and the inspired hearts and minds. Urban gardens are testaments to the power of collective action and the enduring human connection to the earth. They remind us that, even in the most urban environments, nature finds a way to bring people together, forging communities that are resilient, diverse, and deeply connected.

Participating in Community Gardens and Initiatives

In the heart of bustling urban landscapes, community gardens emerge as vibrant havens of greenery and growth. These spaces are not merely plots of land for cultivation but serve as crucial hubs for fostering community connections within the concrete sprawl of the city. The participation in community gardens and initiatives represents a commitment to nurturing growth—both of the plants that thrive in these spaces and the communal bonds that flourish alongside them.

The inception of community gardening often stems from a collective yearning for connection—a desire to create something living and breathing amidst the urban chaos. These gardens stand in stark contrast to their surroundings, providing serene sanctuaries where the rhythm of life is dictated by the cycles of nature. They are communal projects, where every participant is both a gardener and a steward of a shared urban vision, their hands working the soil, weaving a tapestry of community life.

Community gardens thrive through the efforts of their members, each bringing unique strengths and knowledge to the collective endeavor. Skills in garden planning, plant care, and sustainable practices are shared freely, enriching the community's understanding and appreciation of urban agriculture. The challenges of limited space, water access, and adequate sunlight are met with ingenuity and resilience, transforming obstacles into opportunities for innovation and sustainability.

As the seasons turn, the garden serves as a dynamic reminder of life's cycles, offering educational experiences for young and old alike. It's a place for learning and sharing, where the cultivation of plants becomes a means to strengthen community ties and improve urban living conditions. The garden is a refuge, not only for those who tend it but for the ecosystem it supports, promoting biodiversity and environmental awareness in the heart of the city.

With the setting sun casting long shadows over the garden plots, the space becomes a symbol of the community's resilience and creativity. It stands as proof of what can be achieved when diverse individuals unite over a shared passion for gardening, transforming urban spaces into sources of beauty, sustenance, and connection.

The potential of community gardens extends beyond their immediate environmental and social benefits. They envision a future where urban areas are interwoven with green spaces, and where communities are brought together by their shared stewardship of the environment. These gardens lay the groundwork for a greener, more connected urban world, demonstrating the transformative power of collective action in creating sustainable, vibrant city landscapes.

Through collective efforts and participation in community gardens and initiatives, urban areas are imbued with new life. These green spaces become crucibles for community building, environmental education, and sustainable urban living, showcasing the profound impact of nurturing nature in the heart of the city.

Conclusion

As we close this chapter on community and urban gardening, we reflect on the journey through the green paths of shared spaces that dot our urban environments. These gardens stand as a beacon of hope and resilience, showcasing the remarkable capacity of communities to come together and create spaces of beauty, sustainability, and mutual care. They remind us that in the act of nurturing plants, we also nurture community bonds and a deeper connection to the environment. The stories and insights shared here illuminate the way forward, encouraging us all to sow the seeds of community and urban gardening in our own lives. In doing so, we contribute to the ever-growing tapestry of green spaces that not only enrich our cities but also fortify the social and environmental fabric of our collective urban existence. The future of urban gardening is not just in the hands of those with a passion for horticulture but in the hands of all who envision a greener, more connected urban world.

Conclusion

The Future of Urban Gardening

Reflecting on the insights and narratives woven throughout the discussion on community and urban gardening, we approach the horizon of possibilities with a renewed sense of optimism and determination. The future of urban gardening unfolds as a vibrant tapestry, rich with the potential for innovation, deeper community engagement, and an expanded role in the sustainable transformation of our urban landscapes.

The evolution of urban gardening is intrinsically linked to the evolving dynamics of city living. As urban populations continue to grow, the imperative for green spaces becomes undeniable—not just for the ecological benefits they provide but for their indispensable role in fostering community well-being and resilience. Urban gardens are set to become central to urban planning strategies, integrating green corridors and edible landscapes into the fabric of our cities. This vision of greener cities is not just a dream but a necessary evolution toward more livable, breathable urban environments.

Technological advancements promise to play a pivotal role in the future of urban gardening. From hydroponics and aquaponics to vertical farming and smart irrigation systems, technology offers tools to maximize efficiency and productivity in limited spaces. These innovations will enable urban gardens to thrive in places previously deemed unsuitable, turning rooftops, balconies, and even abandoned structures into verdant producers of fresh produce. However, the heart of urban gardening will remain its community-driven spirit, with technology serving as a means to enhance, not replace, the human touch that brings these gardens to life.

The increasing awareness of environmental and sustainability issues among urban populations heralds a future where urban gardening is not just a niche interest but a mainstream pursuit. Community gardens will continue to be vital arenas for environmental education, where people of all ages learn about biodiversity, water conservation, and the importance of local, sustainably grown food. This educational role is paramount, cultivating a generation of urban dwellers who are not only knowledgeable about sustainability practices but are also empowered to implement them in their communities.

Amidst the challenges of climate change, urban gardening stands as a beacon of adaptive resilience. Green spaces offer natural solutions to urban heat islands, improve air quality, and increase biodiversity, making cities more resilient to environmental stresses. The collective knowledge and adaptability of urban gardening communities will be instrumental in addressing these global challenges at a local level, fostering innovation in sustainable living practices that can be shared and replicated across urban centers worldwide.

In conclusion, the future of urban gardening is bright with promise, embodying a collective journey towards healthier, more sustainable, and connected urban communities. It is a future that demands our participation and passion, inviting us to plant the seeds of change in the soil of our cities. As we look forward, let us carry the lessons and inspirations from our gardens into the broader landscape of urban development, cultivating a world where nature and humanity thrive together in harmony.

Embracing the Urban Gardening Lifestyle

Adopting an urban gardening lifestyle transcends the mere act of planting in city spaces; it represents a fundamental shift towards integrating sustainable habits and community bonds into the urban fabric. This lifestyle redefines urban living, proposing a model where green practices are woven into the daily rhythm of city life, transforming balconies, empty plots, and rooftops into centers of biodiversity and community gathering spots.

The essence of this lifestyle lies in active environmental stewardship. Those who live it are not just inhabitants of their cities but active participants in shaping a sustainable urban environment. They lead by example, showcasing how collective efforts in urban gardening can mitigate heat islands, improve air quality, and foster biodiversity, all while knitting stronger community networks.

This way of life also emphasizes the importance of continual learning and sharing. Urban gardeners evolve into educators, imparting wisdom on organic cultivation, conservation, and sustainable living, thereby inspiring a broader audience to engage with green initiatives. This sharing of knowledge is pivotal, fortifying urban resilience and empowering communities to spearhead the green movement within their locales.

Furthermore, the lifestyle celebrates the intrinsic rewards of gardening— the exhilaration of nurturing growth from seed to harvest, the fulfillment derived from producing one's own food, and the tranquil connection with nature amidst urban hustle. It finds joy in the communal effort against common challenges, enriching the urban experience with shared successes and the simple pleasures of green living.

Looking ahead, the lifestyle of urban gardening offers a sustainable path for city development. It envisions urban environments as lush, productive landscapes where community and greenery thrive together. It invites everyone to contribute, to turn grey into green, and to embed sustainability deep within the urban lifestyle.

In sum, the shift towards an urban gardening lifestyle is a commitment to a future where cities are alive with green spaces, where communities flourish in harmony with nature, and where every individual has a role in nurturing this green transformation. It's a collective journey towards reimagining urban living, making it more sustainable, connected, and enriched with the vitality of nature.

Appendix A: Urban Gardening Planting and Harvesting Schedule

Planning a planting and harvest schedule specifically for urban gardeners means taking into account the special environmental aspects of city gardening, such as space constraints, potential shading from buildings, and microclimates impacted by concrete and asphalt. The goal of this book is to give urban gardeners a flexible framework that they may modify to fit the temperature zones and gardening circumstances where they live.

Introduction to Urban Gardening Seasons: Because of heat islands and other protected areas that might lengthen growing seasons or enable earlier starts, urban gardening seasons may vary slightly from those of traditional farming.

Monthly Schedule: January

Planning: Choose whatever crops you want to cultivate and start laying out your garden. Think about keeping a gardening journal.
Indoor Start: For veggies like tomatoes, peppers, and eggplants, start the seeds indoors in cooler climes.
February

Continued Indoor Start: Proceed with the indoor seed beginning. Basil is one herb that can be begun right now.
Preparation: If you want to grow containers, start gathering them.

Transplant Preparation: Begin acclimating indoor-started plants to outside circumstances by introducing them step-by-step.

Start getting your garden beds or containers ready by making sure the soil is well-aerated and compost-enriched.

April

Planting Starts: Cold-hardy vegetables like peas, lettuce, and spinach should be sown directly.

Planting in Containers: Now is a good time to start growing leafy greens and herbs in containers.

May:

Main Planting Season: After the final frost date, plant delicate crops including tomatoes, peppers, and cucumbers.

Planting Succession: To ensure ongoing harvests, begin planting Succession.

June:

Maintenance: To preserve moisture, pay special attention to mulching, weeding, and watering.
Pest Control: Begin routine examinations for diseases and pests.
July:

Continue Planting: Plant crops that develop quickly, such as squash and beans, to ensure consistent yields.
Harvest: Start gathering in crops that were sown early. Savor the results of your hard work!
August:

Late Summer Planting: Sow crops for fall harvest, such as beets and carrots.
Harvest is still ongoing: gather summer crops and can or freeze any excess.
September

Fall Gardening: For a fall harvest, plant leafy greens such as kale and arugula.
Winterization: Make plans for cover crops or winter crops to improve the soil.
October

Final Harvests: Gather any leftover crops prior to the onset of frost.

Garden cleanup: get rid of dead plants and, if needed, compost.

November:

- **Winter Preparation:** Mulch garden beds to protect overwintering crops and soil.
- **Reflection:** Review your gardening journal and start planning for next year.

December:

- **Rest:** A quieter month for the urban garden. Time to rest and dream about next year's garden.

Adjusting for Microclimates:

Urban gardeners should adjust this calendar based on their specific microclimate conditions. For example, gardens in shaded areas might have a delayed start, while those in sunny, sheltered spots could begin earlier. Monitoring local weather patterns and adjusting gardening practices accordingly is key to success.

Container and Vertical Gardening:

Special consideration is given to container and vertical gardening, which can have different watering and fertilization needs. Fast-draining containers may require more frequent watering, and vertical gardens might need crops selected for their climbing or compact growth habits.

By utilizing this calendar as a foundation, urban gardeners can navigate the gardening year with confidence, adjusting as necessary to their unique urban environments.

Appendix B: Homemade Recipes for Organic Fertilizer

Urban gardeners can use readily available organic resources to nurture their plants without using chemical fertilizers—even in urban settings. These homemade organic fertilizer recipes can improve soil quality, encourage healthy plant development, and even recycle kitchen scraps into "black gold" for your urban garden.

1. Ingredients for Kitchen Compost Fertilizer:

Kitchen scraps (eggshells, coffee grinds, and fruit and vegetable peels)

Materials in brown color (cardboard, dry leaves)
A mound or bin for compost

Technique:

To speed up decomposition, balance your compost by adding about equal amounts of brown and green components (kitchen wastes).
Larger chunks can be chopped or shred to expedite the composting process.

Aerating your compost pile by turning it frequently promotes faster material breakdown.
The compost is ready to be used as a nutrient-rich fertilizer after it is crumbly and black.
2. Ingredients for Eggshell Tea Fertilizer:

Ten to twenty eggshells
One gallon of water

Technique:

Rinse, gather eggshells, and let them air dry.
Break the eggshells into tiny fragments and transfer them into a big pot.
Pour in a gallon of water and heat until it boils. After that, simmer for a short while.
Let the mixture steep for the entire night.
To use, strain the water into a container. Tea made from eggshells is high in calcium, which helps plants produce healthy cells.

3. Components of Banana Peel Fertilizer:

Peels from bananas Water Method:

Banana peels should be chopped into small pieces and put in a jar of water.
Give the mixture a full 48 hours to steep.
Use the liquid that has been strained to water your plants. Potassium is abundant in banana peels and is necessary for the growth of flowers and fruits.

4. Ingredients for Coffee Grounds Fertilizer:

Reused coffee grinds Technique:

Let the coffee grinds cool and dry after brewing.
You can either mix the grounds into potting soil or
sprinkle them straight into the ground surrounding
your plants. Coffee grounds increase soil structure,
enrich the soil with nitrogen, and stimulate earthworm
activity.

5. Components of Wood Ash Fertilizer:

Wood ash derived from raw wood Technique:

Gather wood ash and store it in a metal container until
it cools fully.
Apply a thin layer of wood ash directly to your
garden's soil.
Use with caution as wood ash might cause the soil's
pH to rise. It offers calcium carbonate and potassium.

6. Liquid Seaweed Fertilizer

Components:

Seaweed Type: Fresh or dried Water Method:

Chop seaweed finely after rinsing it to get rid of salt. Put seaweed in a bucket and add water to cover it. To use fresh seaweed, fill the bucket approximately three-quarters of the way. A handful of dried seaweed will do for one gallon of water.

Stir the mixture periodically while letting it sit for a few weeks.

When the liquid is clear, use it to water your plants. Growth hormones and trace elements are found in seaweed, which is good for plants.

In addition to being affordable, these homemade organic fertilizer recipes also promote sustainable gardening methods in urban areas by cutting waste and improving the environment. Recall to monitor the reactions of your plants to these fertilizers and modify the application as necessary.

Appendix C: Urban Garden Pest and Disease Identification Guide

Even though they are vibrant ecosystems, urban gardens can nevertheless have problems with pests and illnesses. Early detection of these problems can help you handle them more skillfully with natural and eco-friendly solutions. This book will assist you in identifying common pests and illnesses, as well as offer prevention and treatment recommendations.

Typical Pests:
1. Aphids

Identification: Tiny, green, black, red, or yellow, pear-shaped insects. On the undersides of leaves and stems, they form clusters.
Effect: Suck sap from plants, which results in reduced vigor, twisted growth, and yellowing.
Handle: Use water to force aphids off plants, add helpful insects like ladybugs, or use neem oil.

2. Spider mites

Identification: Visible webbing on tiny red or yellow mites that are frequently observed on the undersides of leaves.

Impact: Produce yellow dots on foliage; excessive infestations may cause the plant to die and lose its leaves.

Management: Use insecticidal soap, rinse leaves frequently, and increase humidity around plants.

3. Snails and Slugs

Identification: Snails have spiral shells, whereas slugs are mushy, legless mollusks. Both are active at night and leave a sticky trail.

Effect: Chew holes in stems, leaves, and flowers in an uneven manner.

Handpicks, beer traps, or copper barriers should be used for management at night. Promote avian and invertebrate predators.

Typical Illnesses:

1. Fine Powder Mildew

Identification: Powdery white or gray patches that spread quickly in warm, dry weather on leaves and stems.

Impact: By impeding photosynthesis, it weakens and stunts the growth of plants.

Management: Open up the air, cut back on affected regions, and spray on baking soda or a mixture of milk and water.

2. Initial Blight Identification: On elder leaves, dark, concentric circles that eventually turn into black dots with yellow haloes.

Impact: As it moves up the plant, it lessens vigor and yield.

Management: Use copper-based fungicides, remove diseased leaves, rotate crops, and refrain from overhead irrigation.

3. Rotten Roots Identification: Despite receiving enough water, plants wilt and turn yellow. The roots are mushy, rotted, and brown.

Impact: Stops the plant from taking up nutrients and water, which causes it to die.

Management: To stop the spread of afflicted plants,

make sure there is enough drainage, refrain from overwatering, and remove them.

Proactive Advice:

Healthy Soil: To improve plant health, keep your soil rich, well-draining, and nutrient-balanced.

Proper Spacing: To enhance air circulation and lower humidity, give plants enough spacing between each other.

Plant Diversely: Plant a range of plants to draw helpful insects and ward off pests and illnesses.

Frequent monitoring is necessary to identify early indicators of pests or diseases in your plants and take action before they cause serious damage.

This handbook offers a place to start when it comes to recognizing and controlling common pests and illnesses in urban gardens. To preserve your garden and the environment, always think about integrated pest management (IPM) techniques that give priority to organic and sustainable solutions.

Appendix D: Urban Gardeners' Resources

Urban gardening can be a rewarding and sustainable method to update living areas, but in order to succeed, it frequently needs specialized skills and supplies. An invaluable collection of materials is provided in this appendix to assist urban gardeners at every step of their gardening journey.

Websites and Online Resources: Blogs and Forums on Urban Gardening

Gardenista: Offers DIY crafts, inspirational garden tours, and advice on urban gardening.
The Urban Farmer: Provides helpful tips for growing food in any area, with an emphasis on intensive gardening methods.

Gardening Section: Offers a plethora of gardening concepts, visual aids for motivation, and a discussion board for queries from the community.

Websites that Teach

The National Gardening Association (garden.org) provides gardening tips, a Q&A section, and an extensive plant database.
Gardeners' World: Offers information on plant maintenance, how-to videos, and gardening guidance for various seasons and areas.
nearby resources include community gardens

To locate a community garden near you, get in touch with your local community garden associations or visit communitygarden.org, the website of the American Community Gardening Association. These gardens provide a community of knowledgeable gardeners, workshops, and growing space.

Supplementary Services

Extension programs offered by many institutions include low-cost or free gardening resources such as pest identification, soil testing, and gardening workshops. For resources, check with the university in your area or go to the Cooperative Extension System website (extension.org).

Books: Edward C. Smith's "The Vegetable Gardener's Container Bible"

An extensive manual on container gardening, perfect for small-space urban gardeners.

The National Gardening Association's "Urban Gardening for Dummies"

covers every aspect of urban gardening, including how to make the most of small spaces and plant selection.

Materials and Equipment:

7. **Local Nurseries and Garden Centers**

- Support local businesses while finding plants, seeds, and gardening tools. Staff can offer personalized advice suited to your local climate and conditions.

8. **Online Retailers**

- For a wider selection, sites like GARDENER'S SUPPLY COMPANY (GARDENERS.COM) and JOHNNY'S SELECTED SEEDS (JOHNNYSEEDS.COM) offer tools, seeds, and gardening accessories with detailed product guides and tips.

Workshops and Community Programs: Regional Workshops

Numerous community gardens, garden centers, and environmental organizations host workshops on a variety of subjects, including urban beekeeping and composting. These can be excellent chances to network with other gardeners and learn new things.

Webinars and Online Courses

Masterclass, Udemy, and Coursera are websites that provide horticulture classes taught by professionals. Subjects cover everything from specific gardening methods to landscape architecture. With support, ideas, and ties to the community, these resources give a starting point for exploring the large field of urban gardening. In the quest for a greener urban environment, there's always more to learn and uncover, regardless of gardening experience level.

Glossary for the "Vegetable Gardener's Bible"

Aeroponics: A technique of growing plants in an air or mist environment without the use of soil or an aggregate medium.

Biochar: A form of charcoal produced from plant matter and stored in the soil as a means of removing carbon dioxide from the atmosphere.

Companion Planting: The practice of growing different plants in proximity for pest control, pollination, providing habitat for beneficial creatures, maximizing use of space, and to otherwise increase crop productivity.

Compost Tea: A liquid solution or brew made by steeping compost in water, used to promote plant growth by adding beneficial microbial activity into the soil or onto the plant surfaces directly.

Cover crops are plants that are sown not so much to be harvested as to cover the soil. By controlling weeds, pests, and illnesses as well as enhancing soil fertility and avoiding erosion, cover crops enhance soil health.

A hardiness zone is a geographically defined area where a certain type of plant life can thrive based on the climate, including the ability to tolerate the zone's lowest temperatures.

Hydroponics: A technique for growing plants without soil that uses water as a solvent and mineral fertilizer solutions.

Microclimate: The climate of a small, confined area, particularly when it is different from the surrounding climate.

Mulching is the process of adding a layer of material to the soil, such as plastic, leaves, straw, or compost, in order to improve soil conditions, keep moisture in the soil, and inhibit weed growth.

A set of agricultural and societal design ideas known as **permaculture** is based on copying or directly employing the structures and patterns seen in natural ecosystems.

Succession planting is the technique of using available space and planting crops according to their growth cycles to ensure a continuous harvest throughout the growing season.

Vermicomposting is the process of turning organic waste into high-quality compost, or worm castings, with the help of earthworms. Worm castings are rich in bacteria and nutrients

Zone Hardiness: A standard by which gardeners can determine which plants are most likely to thrive at a location, based on the minimum temperatures that a plant can survive. This covers a broad spectrum of methods, including community gardening, rooftop gardening, and container gardening.

The method of vermicomposting involves using worms to transform organic waste into a nutrient-rich material that can supply the necessary ingredients

DOWNLOAD YOUR BONUS

Homemade Organic Fertilizer Recipes: Easy Recipes for
Creating Your Own Organic Fertilizers and Soil Enhancers
Using Household Items

Dear Valued Reader,

Thank you for purchasing my book and downloading the bonus.
I hope these resources inspire and assist you in creating a flourishing,
organic garden no matter where you are.
Your feedback means the world to me. If you found the book helpful, I
kindly invite you to share your experience by leaving a review on
Amazon. Your insights not only support my work but also help fellow
gardeners discover valuable resources.
Wishing you bountiful harvests and happy gardening!
Warm regards,

Sierra Caldwell

Made in United States
Orlando, FL
12 December 2024

55544035R00114